MW01136169

Notes

on

Mediumship

Ruth Kidson

Norfolk: Sphinx House Publishing

Published by Sphinx House Publishing, Norfolk

© Ruth Kidson 2019

Book Typesetting & Cover Setup by Velin@Perseus-Design.com

ISBN: 978-1-9997107-3-6

For Mary Hykel Hunt who helped me take
my first faltering steps on this path and
encouraged me to persevere.
And for Michaele Wynn-Jones who first
suggested I do a course at AFC.

A NOTE ON THE LANGUAGE

When referring to sitters, mediums and spirit communicators I have used 'he' and 'she' randomly and, I hope, equally. This is in order to prevent the reader from becoming irritated by a constant repetition of 'he or she' and to stop me from becoming irritated at having to use the ungrammatical 'they'.

TABLE OF CONTENTS

INTRODUCTION

Over the past eleven years I have attended a large number of courses in mediumship at the Arthur Findlay College and elsewhere and have had the privilege of being taught by some of the finest teachers in the world. This book is based on what I have learned on those courses and in classes on SNUi (the online branch of the Spiritualist National Union), together with my own experiences.

I am always impressed by the number of people who travel great distances to go to AFC. I've had the pleasure of meeting visitors from Australia, New Zealand, Japan, Iceland, South America, Canada and the USA as well as from many European countries. But, as prices rise, the cost of courses has become prohibitive for some people - particularly those living outside the UK. This book is in no way a substitute for attending a course, but I hope it may prove useful to those who, for whatever reason, are unable to go to AFC.

Courses at AFC are divided into groups, each with its own tutor. But students come together for talks or workshops from the other tutors on the course. While different aspects of mediumship may be emphasised by different teachers, and while - inevitably - there may be disagreement about the best way to work, many tutors teach along much the same lines. For this reason, individual teachings in the book are, on the whole, not attributed to any one

1

tutor or group of tutors. Nonetheless, I would like to acknowledge all those from whom I have learned:

Eileen Davies   Eamonn Downey
Simone Key   Sheila French
Sandie Baker   Ron Jordan
Matthew Smith   Mallory Stendall
John Johnson   Su Wood
Kitty Woud

whose groups I have been in (some, on several occasions) and:

Colin Bates   Chris Drew
Leah Bond   Libby Clark
Sharon Harvey   Helen Da Vita
Lynn Cottrell   Jose Medrado
Glyn Edwards   Angie Morris
Andrew Manship   Maureen Murnan
Lynn Probert   Scott Milligan
Paul Jacobs   Thelma Francis
Tony Stockwell

whose talks and workshops I have had the pleasure of attending. The wisdom in this book is entirely theirs. Any mistakes are mine alone.

1
WORKING PSYCHICALLY

WHY WORK PSYCHICALLY?

Most evidential mediumship courses at AFC tend to include some psychic development exercises. A number of first-time students are surprised by this – they may have already done a lot of psychic work, or may have been sitting in circles where the focus is purely on mediumship. And a few may consider that, in some way, working psychically is inferior to working as a medium.

But as Simone Key tells her students, if you want to be good medium, you need to be a good psychic. One is not superior to the other. In both you are interacting with the energies of someone else, the difference being that, as a psychic, you are working with someone who is still here on earth and, as a medium, you are working with someone who has passed to spirit.

It's also important to recognise that a lot of people who go to see mediums don't want to contact loved ones in spirit (their loved ones may all still be here!) but they want guidance on what to do at a particularly difficult stage in their lives.

There are many different ways to do a psychic reading (although, in all cases, you will be reading the client's energy). For example, you can look at her aura, or you can read her name, or you can use tarot or oracle cards. And, depending on why it is that she's come to see you, the information you get from working in this way can be of more value to the recipient than a mediumistic contact would be.

One important form of psychic reading is a spiritual assessment in which the information received psychically is combined with guidance from the sitter's guides. Spiritual assessments are valuable for those people who are already developing their spiritual gifts, whether it be a form of mediumship, psychic work, or healing, and can give guidance on the best route for the recipient to take – for example, demonstrating or teaching.

Another reason why we need to learn to work psychically is that it will enable us to develop a better understanding of different types of people who have had a variety of different experiences so that, when we encounter similar types and similar experiences in spirit, we will be able to work more easily with them. This can result in a wider range of people coming through in our mediumship – after all, we don't want to work with grandmothers all the time!

THE DIFFERENCE BETWEEN WORKING PSYCHICALLY AND WORKING MEDIUMISTICALLY

The ability to know when we're working psychically and when we're working mediumistically is a very important one. As already stated, when we work psychically we are getting our information from tuning into the energies, or aura, of our sitter. Working mediumistically, we are getting our information from spirit.

What makes things difficult is that it's quite possible to give what appears to be a mediumistic reading while actually working psychically. For example, in my aura are all the memories I have of my mother – and so a psychic could describe her and perhaps even talk about some of the things we used to do together. But it would only be a description. In order for the full personality of the person in spirit to come through, the medium has to be truly in contact with that person.

So how can you tell the difference when you're the one doing the reading? To me (and to many other mediums I've talked to), a psychic connection feels different from a mediumistic connection. I know this sounds vague and, quite honestly, the best way to understand it is to experience it. All I can say is that, in my case, the information comes in at a different place – psychic energy comes in from directly in front of me (understandable because that's usually where the sitter is) while information from spirit comes in from the left hand side.

A less mumbo-jumbo way of distinguishing the two has been suggested by Tony Stockwell who says that if you're talking about the person in spirit but all you're giving is a description – if you can't feel her personality – if you can't, in a certain sense, become her – then the chances are that you're working psychically.

A useful exercise, if you're still not sure, is to give a psychic reading to a friend and try to feel how the information is reaching you. Then bring in a spirit communicator and allow yourself to become aware of the difference.

DEVELOPING PSYCHIC ABILITIES

When I first became interested in working with spirit, I spent five years in a psychic development group before joining a circle and starting to go to courses at AFC. For me, this worked well as I needed to build my confidence in my psychic abilities before I tried to make contact with spirit. But it's an individual thing and it's perfectly possible to train in both areas at the same time – just don't ignore the psychic!

Whether we are working psychically or mediumistically, it is always important to trust what we get. The more we can trust our own abilities, the stronger those abilities will become. However, at the beginning, it's not easy and I remember, when I started going to a psychic development group, I would frequently put up the plaintive cry "I'm not getting anything!" Our tutor, Mary Hykel Hunt, had a wonderful way round this. "OK," she'd say, "You're not getting anything. But if you were getting something – what would it be?" That little phrase has stood me in good stead and I recommend it to you. It takes you outside your anxieties of not being able to get anything and, almost invariably, allows you to start getting information.

Three objects

In the psychic development group, one of the first exercises I was taught was the 'three objects reading'. You ask the person you're reading for to look round the room (or rooms) you're working in and pick out three objects that she feels drawn to. Then you read them.

The first time I did it, the person I was working with picked up a small crystal, a matchbox and half a lemon. I can't remember how I interpreted the crystal but I remember noticing that the matchbox said on its label "wipe clean cover" and I suggested that my sitter tended to keep her emotions (represented by the matches and the fire they create) inside her, underneath a pristine veneer. I remember, too, that the lemon made me think of the sun, brightness, joy and hope which indicated that my sitter was starting to find ways of opening up. All of which she confirmed as being true.

This exercise is best done with someone you don't know too well, to stop your own knowledge intruding on what you're picking up psychically.

THE AURA

When we work psychically, we are linking into the sitter's aura, which holds information about all aspects of our lives, experiences and health. The aura is said to have seven layers, each being linked to one of the chakras or energy centres. Starting closest to the body, the layers are the:

- Etheric – linked to the base chakra
- Emotional – linked to the sacral chakra
- Mental – linked to the solar plexus chakra
- Astral – linked to the heart chakra
- Spiritual – linked to the throat chakra
- Celestial – linked to the brow chakra (or third eye)
- Ketheric – linked to the crown chakra

When encountering aura reading for the first time, many people say "But I don't see auras." The answer is – you don't have to. Although some people are able to see the etheric layer visually, none of the others is visible to the eyes and aura reading is done simply by sensing the energies and interpreting them. So, when I describe part of a sitter's aura as royal blue, for example, it's because the energies of that part of the aura are translating themselves in my mind into that colour and that, in turn, is giving me information about what is going on there. It would be possible, of course, to get the information directly but using colour makes it easier.

The etheric body is the layer most closely connected to the physical body, and reflects the health of the sitter. It is the only layer of the aura that can be seen (by some people) with the naked eye. Years ago, a friend of mine, hearing about the aura for the first time, was astonished to discover that the "half inch of shimmering" which she had always seen round people (and that she assumed everyone else saw as well) was, in fact, their etheric body.

The emotional body reflects a person's emotions and feelings and is constantly changing, as his moods change. Its proximity to the etheric body explains in part why emotions can rapidly create or exacerbate physical symptoms (for example asthma, irritable bowel syndrome or migraine). The mental body reflects the person's thoughts and ideas. In my experience, reading this layer inevitably involves reading the emotional body as well, to give a full picture of the sitter's mental processes.

The astral layer is related to feelings of love and balance in a person's life. It is the midway point between the inner three layers (which relate to the body) and the outer three (which relate to the spirit).

These outer three layers – the spiritual layer, the celestial layer and the ketheric template – enable us to connect to the Divine through meditation or other spiritual practice and they hold the record of our spiritual development.

Although they are described as layers, it is important to remember that, being energy fields, the seven layers permeate each other and the physical body too. They are said to be a few inches to a few feet thick but they can be expanded by spiritual practice. The Buddha is said to have had an aura that was three miles wide. Bearing in mind that I've just said that we can only see the innermost layer, you may be wondering how anyone knew this. Well, of course, they may have seen his aura psychically, but I think it's more likely that they felt it. There are some people who make you feel good as you get nearer to them – in other words, as you step into their aura. The Buddha's aura would have conveyed a sense of peace, compassion and loving-kindness long before you got close to him.

I have been told that every time Gordon Higginson (1918-1993) – one of the finest mediums of the twentieth century – arrived at Arthur Findlay College, people would be aware that he was in the building, not because they had seen him but because they could feel his energy.

So, when we read an aura, we are using our senses rather than our eyes. However, my own experience tells me that our eyes do, in some way, register the aura. I am a medical hypnotherapist and, years ago, soon after I'd finished my training, I offered to treat a friend who suffered from migraine. Her husband was sitting in the room with us and it was he who pointed out to me that – even though he knew nothing about hypnosis – he could tell the exact moment when his wife went into a hypnotic trance, because her aura shrank down. Once he'd pointed that out to me, I started to use it as an additional indication that a patient had gone into hypnosis – and it's been very useful. What the difference is, I can't say precisely, other than the fact that someone in hypnosis looks subtly different from someone who is not in a state of trance. This is also a useful thing to bear in mind when people ask whether hypnosis and meditation work in much the same way. The answer, for me, is no, they can't do – because hypnosis contracts the aura, while meditation expands it.

There are a number of books around on aura reading that focus on its colours and how to interpret them. And, indeed, allowing yourself to receive impressions of the energies in someone's aura as colours is a good way of working. However, it's really important that you then interpret those colours according to what you feel they mean, rather than using the stock interpretations in the books. For example, yellow may mean sunshine or spring to a person who loves that colour. But to someone who dislikes the colour or has had bad experiences around it, it may suggest something quite different. Remember that the colours you see in an aura are not real colours but, rather, your mind's interpretation of certain energies. In addition, there are different shades of colour – a dark blue may convey something quite different from a pale blue. And a colour you see in one person's aura may not mean the same thing in someone else's. When I see red, for example, it might mean love, or anger, or passion, or determination or something else entirely.

READING THE AURA

When we read the aura, we read only the physical aura (the etheric layer), the mental aura, the emotional aura and the spiritual aura, in that order.

Everything about a person is held in his or her aura. You can see what has happened in the past as well as what is happening in the present and, when reading, it's important to be aware of this. Remember, too, that something traumatic that happened in childhood may still be having repercussions and so may span a long period of the sitter's life.

With practice you will find that you can get a great deal of information from the aura. For example, you may become aware that the sitter is a healer but you can then take this further to see where her skills lie – is she a spiritual healer, a Reiki practitioner, an acupuncturist, a nurse – or perhaps a doctor? Reading at this sort of depth is important when you are doing a spiritual assessment and you are looking at the areas on which the sitter would do well to concentrate – for example, demonstrating, private sittings, trance or teaching.

Deficiencies may also be apparent in someone's aura. You can look to see whether there are colours that the sitter needs in order to balance her energies better and you can discuss how she might bring these into her life – for example, by wearing these colours or by introducing them into her decor at home.

INFORMATION FROM THE DIFFERENT LAYERS OF THE AURA

The physical or etheric layer will give you information about the sitter's personality and temperament. You will also be able to gauge his energy level and get an indication of his state of health. You may become aware that he has been having problems with a particular part of the body – such as backache or toothache.

From the mental layer you can assess the sitter's level of education, the work he does, the hobbies he enjoys. You can also look at whether he is creative (and how he expresses it – is he a writer, actor, painter, gardener?). Does he have any particular fears or phobias or is he a very logical and down to earth person? And you can also see what is uppermost in his mind at the moment, such as money worries or concerns about work or a relationship.

The emotional level will tell you about the sitter's interaction with other people – his family, colleagues and friends. You may become aware of his marital status and of whether he has children.

The spiritual aura is read in depth in a spiritual assessment but should be touched on in any aura reading. It will give an indication of the sitter's pathway through life, of any psychic abilities she may possess and where these might take her.

Practising aura reading

This is best done with someone you don't know intimately. Allow yourself to 'focus out' and then feel her energies. This is something we do every day without being aware of it – we know if someone is agitated or angry or happy or peaceful without them having to tell us. How does your sitter feel?

Concentrate first on the physical aura. All you need to do is to put out the intention of picking up the relevant energies. Is your sitter full of energy or feeling tired or somewhere in between? Does she have any aches or pains and, if so, how does she react to them – does she ignore them, does she feel sorry for herself? This can take you into her personality – does she tend usually to be optimistic and cheerful or is she always waiting for the worst to happen . . . or is she somewhere in between?

When you've got as much as you can from the physical level, go on to the mental. Is your sitter a thinker? A chatterbox? Does she like to read – if so, what sort of thing? Does she have an enquiring mind? What does she enjoy doing? Is anything worrying her?

Going on to the emotional level – who is she close to? How does she interact with people? Is she shy or outgoing? Does she make friends easily? You may pick up details of relationships with specific members of the family. Do remember to word your information carefully. Telling someone that she and her husband fight like cat and dog is unlikely to go down well. "You and your husband sometimes have differences of opinion" is probably a more acceptable way of putting it. Similarly, "I feel that you don't have a close relationship with your mother" is better than "you haven't spoken to your mother in five years".

Finally, have a look at the spiritual aura. There may not be very much there to read. Just because someone has come for a reading doesn't necessarily mean that she is on a spiritual path. You may, however, see that she has some spiritual beliefs or spiritual abilities. I know a number of psychics and mediums who started their development after a reading in which they were told that they had latent abilities.

Rather than just feel the energies, some people find it easier to use colours. Start by unfocusing your eyes and then allowing yourself to picture the colours in each section of the aura – physical, mental, emotional and spiritual.

Another, more in-depth, way of reading the aura is to read each of the four layers in different periods of the person's life – for example, childhood, teens and twenties, and thirties onwards. I remember doing this exercise at AFC and being asked, before we started, to choose a colour for each of the periods. Looking at my sitter (who was in her early thirties) I chose red for her childhood, blue for her teens and silver for twenty onwards. I started by concentrating on the red at each of the four levels and then I repeated this with the blue and finally with the silver. Working in this way, I found that a huge amount of information was available to me.

Using colours to read auras doesn't work for everybody but, if you are someone who is particularly aware of colour (and, particularly, if you tend to dream in colour) you may find that using colour in your work will enable you to read energies more accurately.

THE ETHICS OF PSYCHIC READING

You should never read someone's aura without his permission. To read it without his knowledge or consent would be intrusive and akin to reading his personal diary or letters. So if someone asks you to read her partner or a colleague, tell her that, even though you can understand how it might be helpful in the situation that she has described, you cannot do it without that partner or colleague's consent.

One exception to this is in name reading and numerology where it is considered acceptable to read the name or numbers of someone who is in the public eye (such as a politician or actor) or of someone who has passed into spirit.

Another very important factor to remember is that, even though you can get health information from the physical layer, you cannot – and, indeed, must not – try to diagnose or prescribe treatments. Firstly, if you tell a client that he has a particular illness and it turns out not to be the case, it is likely that you will have caused him a great deal of distress. And secondly, if the stress has been severe, the client may decide to sue you. And if you're not a doctor he is likely to win the case. Even if you are a doctor (as am I) you're on very shaky ground if the sole reason for your diagnosis is what you have seen in the client's aura.

If you do see something that troubles you in the physical aura, there are ways of expressing it without alarming the client. For example, if you see something in the digestive system you could say "I'm getting a sense that you've been having some problems in your abdomen". If the client admits that this is so, but hasn't sought medical advice, say something along the lines of "Well, it might be a good idea to have a word with your doctor. There's no point in putting up with something if you don't have to."

You also need to be very careful if a sitter asks you for advice based on what you have seen in the aura, and you must always make it clear that you are only offering a suggestion. You cannot tell people what they should do. The choice must always remain theirs. Equally, your suggestions should never be intrusive and must always be constructive. So, for example, if you pick up psychically that a client is unhappy in her marriage (or if she tells you this), while it might be acceptable to suggest that she finds a counsellor to whom she can talk about this, it would never be acceptable to suggest that she leaves her husband. Remember that the vast majority of your clients will be vulnerable in some respect so you have to be very careful about how you express yourself.

It is also important to remember that you cannot always provide what the sitter wants. A number of people go to see mediums or psychics because they want their fortunes told. This is particularly so with tarot reading. When I read tarot, I always explain it as being like a road map – it shows where you are at the moment, the possible roads that you can take, any difficulties you might encounter along the way, and where you might end up if you take a particular route. But the choice is always yours. You can take a completely different route, or you can stay where you are, or you can try one route and then come back and try another. The future is not set in stone and we should never give a client the impression that it is. If someone specifically wants her fortune told (often this is along the lines of "when will I meet my future husband?" or "will I win the lottery?"), apologise and tell her that you don't work that way. She can then decide whether to leave or to stay and have the sort of reading that you do provide.

Whatever information you give a sitter (and this applies to mediumistic readings as well as psychic), it must always be uplifting and constructive. For example, if you are doing a reading for someone who wants to become a healer and you can't see healing in his aura, do not tell him that he can't be a healer. It may be that you just can't see it rather than that it's not there. Or it may be something that he will develop at some time in the future. Instead, look to see what skills are there and talk about those. Maybe he is psychic, in which case you could justifiably suggest that for the time being it will be more beneficial to his spiritual work to concentrate on this.

Most of us, I think, will have heard stories of people being given 'bad news' by psychics or mediums. One woman I know was told, in her twenties, that she would die from breast cancer when she was 63. Although she put this to the back of her mind, it clearly niggled in her subconscious because it became a self-fulfilling prophecy and, at the age of 63, she developed breast cancer. However, by then, she had done a lot of psychic development and was aware that the rest of the prediction didn't have to come true if she didn't want it to. She used a variety of complementary therapies together with orthodox treatment and has now been clear of cancer for some fifteen years.

The results of a negative prediction are not always this dramatic. However, a person who is told that he will die at the age of thirty four is likely to become very resentful and distressed when he reaches thirty five and realises how much time he has spent worrying about the prediction. Even then, he may not be free of anxiety but may start to think "maybe she meant forty four . . . or fifty four . . ." No one has the right to put anxieties into someone's mind that do not need to be there.

A SHORT NOTE ON PSYCHOMETRY

When we have owned or used an object for a long time, it will pick up our energies, which can then be read psychically. It is customary for the reader to hold the object and then talk about the person who owns (or owned) it. It takes a long time for something to lose the energy of the person who has owned it so, if the object has been owned by a number of people, the energies may be blurred and it is best to concentrate on those of the person to whom it belonged most recently. However, if the present owner has only had it for a short time, the energies of one or more previous owners may be stronger. It is therefore important, if you are offering this type of reading, to ask the client to bring something that he has had for several years and either wears or uses fairly regularly.

A good way to practise psychometry is to ask a group of friends each to put one object into a bag. You then pick out one at a time, not knowing who it belongs to, and read it.

Hold the object in the palm of your hand – there is an energy centre (or minor chakra) there and this will enable you to pick up the energies of the object more easily. Try to rid yourself of any preconceptions. If, for example, you pick a man's watch from the bag, don't assume that it belongs to a man. Some women prefer big watches – or it may have belonged to the owner's father or uncle.

Sometimes it's easiest to start by feeling what, if anything, is special about the object – was it a gift from someone close (if so, who?). Did it belong to a relative or friend of the current owner? Or is it something that the owner bought for himself? Then feel the intensity of the owner's energy in the object. Is it something he has owned for a long time and uses frequently? Or does it sit in a drawer most of the time? If the object has only been in the person's possession for a short time, you may not get very much – in which case you can say that you feel it's a recent purchase, or gift or bequest (whichever seems right). Then see what the object is telling you about its owner.

A SHORT NOTE ON NAME READING

The name we are given at birth may not be one we're comfortable with – I know several people who use their middle name rather than their first name. And, of course, many women change their surname when they marry. It is normally considered best to read the energies of the name as it appears on the birth certificate but, in my experience, any name which the person considers to be his or her own can be read with some accuracy.

Some years ago I went through the Tibetan Buddhist ceremony of 'taking precepts' and was given a Tibetan name. I've never been called by that name but because of how it was bestowed, I acknowledge it as being mine. A while back, I was teaching a psychic development class and we were doing name reading. As an experiment, I put my Tibetan name up on the board and asked the students to read it. No one knew that it was my name, nor even that it belonged to a Westerner. And because it was Tibetan, no one knew if the owner of the name was male or female. But every student who read it came up with a recognisable description of my personality and lifestyle.

There are various ways to read names but, ultimately, it's the same as any psychic exercise – you are picking up the energies associated with that name. You can look psychically for colours or shapes suggested by the name, or look at what the parts of the name suggest to you (for example, the surname 'Wingate' can be divided into 'win' and 'gate', while 'Henshaw' gives 'hen' and 'shaw' which sounds the same as 'shore' and 'sure', and so on). Or you can feel for the energies in the name. There's no set way of doing it - experiment and see what works for you.

2
MEDIUMS AND MEDIUMSHIP

WHAT IS MEDIUMSHIP?

We tend to think of mediumship as being simply about getting messages from spirit or, as some people would express it, "talking to dead people". But it's much more than that. Kitty Woud has described it as being a mystical pathway that ultimately leads to God. Its purpose is to touch and awaken our souls and, in so doing, to touch the souls of others.

True mediumship should be healing and uplifting, and a service to both humanity and to spirit. What you say to people, as a medium, will stay with them. Negative ideas can cause untold harm, whereas positive thoughts can bring about turning points and change people's lives.

You can't become a medium overnight – there are no tricks, secrets or shortcuts. And, while you can improve your mediumship by learning different techniques, you first have to commit to developing yourself and to forming a relationship with spirit.

CAN ANYONE BE A MEDIUM?

Opinions differ on this. Some people say yes but only up to a point. It's rather like singing – most people can sing, even if it's just in the bath, but very few will become opera stars. One AFC tutor suggested that probably only one person in 10,000 has true mediumistic ability, and only one in 100,000 will go on to realise his or her potential.

However, it seems that everyone is born with psychic ability, although most people lose this when, at school, emphasis is put on working with the left brain (logic, thinking and learning) at the expense of the right brain (intuition and creativity). The good news, though, is that it's perfectly possible, with training, to recover your psychic abilities and to put them to good use.

And, of course, everyone has the ability to communicate with the Divine Source, even if they're not mediums. Anything which involves working with compassion – such as nursing, medicine, social work, or being a good parent or a good neighbour – entails a link to the Divine.

If your mediumship manifested itself spontaneously (for example, if you started to hear or to see spirit before you had any training) this is a good indication that you have potential. Because, of course, mediumship is a two way communication – spirit has got to want to communicate through you and if they have already picked you out, and if you respond to the call with a wish to serve, this bodes well for the future. Mediumship is not a job – it's a sacred calling. You need to feel an allegiance to spirit and a desire to serve both spirit and the human race.

People come into mediumship training at different times in their lives. At AFC you will find beginners of all ages, from teenagers to fifties, sixties and even, occasionally, seventies. But it doesn't matter when you come into it as long as it's the right time for you. If you're a late starter, there's no point in thinking "I wish I'd done this years ago." The circumstances might not have been right then or you might not have been ready. My own mediumship first manifested in my early twenties when I started to hear spirit voices. It scared the living daylights out of me and I suppressed it for a long time. It was only later, after having done several years of psychic development, that I felt brave enough to investigate contact with the spirit world.

But medium or not, we can all serve spirit. Gordon Higginson, who taught for many years at AFC, said "The spirit world has an interest in you – go and find out what it is." We need to understand how we work with and interact with spirit and to allow ourselves to be guided. Our initial ideas of what we want to do may not necessarily be what spirit wants us to do. I know of at least one world-class medium who originally wanted to be a healer.

But if it seems that you have mediumistic abilities and you are planning to develop your mediumship, there are three things you need in addition to your committment to spirit – a knowledge of theory, a great deal of practice, and a commitment to self-development.

SELF DEVELOPMENT

Mediumship is not just about demonstrating and giving readings. Personal development is vital, as is self-care. Tony Stockwell has commented that if you set up as a medium without having attended to your own personal development, a difficult client can bring you to your knees.

Development takes place every day, if we allow it to, and while there are some very impressive young mediums, experience of life will always enhance our mediumistic abilities.

Self development also means learning to trust – not just the spirit world but ourselves as well. We need to believe in ourselves and to set the intention to become the best we can be. We also need to get to know ourselves – to learn who we truly are. Because we as people are important. One AFC tutor described the goal of mediumship as being at one with yourself and with all the universe. To focus totally on the spirit world and lose sight of ourselves completely will lead to an imbalance which could be harmful. The greatest mystics may have had their heads in heaven but they also had their feet on the ground.

Learning to love

Eileen Davies teaches that everything comes from a perspective of love or a perspective of fear. Our own energy affects everything we do. Only by approaching mediumship from a place of love can we help the two worlds to come together.

We need to learn to acknowledge that everyone has a spark of the Divine (even though in some it may seem to be well and truly hidden!). We need to be non-judgmental and to accept that we can learn from everyone – even if, with some, we just learn that we don't want to behave as they do.

But love is not just about loving others. We need to learn to recognise the light and the love within ourselves and to allow it to grow. And this means that we need to learn to love ourselves, too. For many people this is not easy as they've been brought up to play down their gifts and achievements. But appreciating yourself is not to do with egotism. You're not standing up and trumpeting your successes to all and sundry. You're not saying you're the greatest person in the world. You're just looking at yourself and acknowledging your good characteristics and the things you have achieved – in exactly the same way that you would appreciate these things in someone else. And, perhaps, even more important, you're forgiving yourself for those things that you would easily forgive in others, acknowledging that, like the rest of the human race, you're not perfect and don't have to be.

In Buddhism there is a meditation practice called mettabhavana which means 'development of loving-kindness'. It consists of sending loving-kindness to those who are dearest to you, then to family and friends who are not quite as close, then to acquaintances and colleagues, then people you meet who you don't really know (the person behind the counter at the post office, the person on the checkout at the supermarket), then to everyone else in the country and finally to everyone else in the world. But right at the start, before you do any of this, you send loving-kindness to yourself because, unless you can learn to love yourself, you cannot truly give love to anyone else.

There is a wonderful poem by Marianne Williamson (once, famously, quoted by Nelson Mandela) in which she says:

"We ask ourselves, who am I to be brilliant, gorgeous, talented and fabulous? .
Actually, who are you not to be?"

As we let our own light shine and learn to love ourselves, we unconsciously give other people permission to do the same for themselves. Liberating ourselves from our own fear means that our presence can allow others to be liberated too.

As we allow our light to grow, it enables us to have a better relationship with God, or the Divine, and this in turn enables us to have a better relationship with our fellow human beings.

Self care

Self care is vital. It's not easy being a working medium, no matter how glamorous it may appear to be. It can also be a lonely road, because not everyone understands or approves of Spiritualism. Finding a good friend to whom you can talk about your spiritual work is invaluable. If you are fortunate enough to be able to go to courses at AFC you will meet people of like mind, and many long term friendships begin there.

While mediumship needs dedication, you also need to know when to step back. You cannot be open to spirit all the time or you will burn out. Be aware of when you need to be quiet and by yourself, and act upon it.

If you're ill or exhausted or you've suffered a bereavement yourself, you should take some time off from mediumship and ask spirit to help you heal.

WHAT MAKES A GREAT MEDIUM?

Having had the privilege of being taught by a number of great mediums over the years, there are certain things that I see they all have in common:
- integrity
- compassion
- humility
- sense of service
- dedication
- and a sense of humour

These characteristics have nothing to do with their mediumship per se – these are personal qualities. We are people first, not mediums, and it is how we live our lives that matters.

All great mediums will tell you that there is always more to learn and always room for improvement. They are still developing, which is why many prefer the term 'unfoldment' rather than 'development', since it suggests a constant process without an end product.

POSITIVE THINKING

At the beginning of many courses at AFC the tutor will ask his or her group what each member wants to gain from the week. In my experience, at least half the group will talk about the need to improve their confidence. So, inevitably, a lot of the teaching is about positive thinking. However, this isn't just about making us feel better and allowing us to enjoy our mediumship more. Positive thoughts produce positive results whereas doubt produces stress and negative energy which can actually repel spirit.

One problem that we all face on a course at AFC, where we are working alongside a large number of other mediums, is that we will all find people who are 'better at it' than we are. Even the experienced working mediums can look at the tutors (who demonstrate in the twice-weekly services) and start to compare themselves with them. If we worry that we are not as good as other people, it can interfere with our own progress. Focusing on *what* we want to be can stop us from becoming what we *could* be.

It is, of course, natural to want to be like the top mediums. But, as John Johnson reminded us: "You can only be you. Everybody else is taken." The important thing is not to have a goal – a 'what I want to achieve' – but, rather, an aspiration to continue to improve, in the knowledge that this is a continual process. The seventh of the seven principles of the Spiritualists' National Union is "Eternal progress open to every human soul". Who knows what we are capable of? On several occasions I have heard Sandie Baker, a very fine medium and tutor, say that she considers herself still to be a beginner.

So how do we increase our sense of positivity and confidence? For some of us (myself included) it's a long process, so a determination to keep going is essential. It's also important to ignore people who try to put us down, who criticise us in ways that aren't constructive, or who ridicule what we are doing. They are only doing that because of their own inadequacies and it makes no sense to allow their deficiencies to affect our progress.

Of course, we may be fortunate enough to have people around us who support us in what we're doing. But, even so, we have to guard against being over-critical of ourselves. If we tell ourselves "I'll never be good enough", or "I'll never be as good as X", we won't be. We need to recognise our own abilities, remembering that it's pointless to think about what we might or might not do in the future. What matters is what's happening now.

If you sit regularly in a circle, it's helpful to keep a journal and make notes after each session as a reminder of what you have achieved. When you're just starting out, it may be only a little – perhaps simply an awareness of a man or woman in spirit, without much more information. When you begin to get more, record your progress. And record, too, what others have said about your mediumship. I have a very fond memory of a course at AFC some years ago when Sandie Baker, having seen me demonstrate, commented "You couldn't have done that two years ago."

On a recent course, Colin Bates advised us not to tell ourselves that we *want* to be good mediums or that we will be good mediums but, rather, to believe that we are good mediums. This is not egotistical – it is a desire to do well. We should do everything well, he continued: "Be fab – and, even if you get something wrong, be fab in your wrongness!"

Never give up on wishes and dreams because you may be closer to realising them than you think. Trust spirit, and spirit will support you. Tell spirit what it is you are trying to do. But do be open to their guidance. There will always be one facet of your mediumship that is better than the others and it's no good deciding that you'd rather do something else. If your skill is in healing, for example, focus on that and be as good at it as you possibly can, and leave the demonstrating to those who don't have your healing abilities.

Creating inner balance, peace and harmony through concentrating on positivity and coming from a place of love and not fear will lead to the progress that you desire. If you believe you can do it, you will. The only obstacle is if you think you can't.

DEDICATION AND ATTITUDE

If you seriously want to be a medium, you need to be dedicated. Mediumship has to be worked at. Not only do we need to work continuously on our self-development, increasing in love, compassion, understanding and patience but we also need to find the time to practise blending with spirit.

If our motivation is right and we are approaching our development with a spiritual purpose, this will help to bring balance and harmony into our lives. However, we do need to retain just a touch of ego, in that we need to be confident that we will succeed.

This is probably the hardest thing for beginners – and sometimes even for more experienced mediums – to do. We tend to doubt ourselves. And, in so doing, we doubt spirit. We question the information we're getting. We start to wonder "Is this coming from spirit or is it me?" and so make it harder for ourselves because, instead of getting our minds out of the process and just accepting the information that comes in, we are bringing our minds more firmly into it, and so impeding the flow.

We worry that we're making it up because, in everyday life, when we're using our imaginations, that's exactly what we are doing. But, for most of us – those who aren't so clairaudient that they hear spirit voices outside themselves – imagination is the way that spirit communicates with us.

I remember, a number of years ago, Sharon Harvey running a workshop at AFC and taking a very nervous beginner onto the platform. She asked him to link to spirit and then to make up a story about a person, without worrying where he was getting it from. "Is your story about a man or a woman?" she asked. He chose a woman. "How old is she?" He gave an age. "Where does she live?" He named a particular part of England. After he had given several specific pieces of information, Sharon asked if anyone could recognise this woman. One person could – and could take all the information. But the lad on the platform had thought he was making it all up.

As we become more experienced, it is easier to tell whether or not the information is coming from spirit. If it flows and we're speaking fluently, we're likely to be in the power and receiving the information from spirit. If we're floundering or searching for things to say, or if a piece of information doesn't 'feel right', it's likely to be coming from our own minds.

But if we trust to spirit and, in effect, hand the process over to them, it makes it much easier. One way of doing this is to commit ourselves to being the best we can, not for ourselves, but for spirit.

Anxiety can be a negative force and, while a certain 'edge' is good thing (as any performer will tell you) abject terror is not and will form a barrier that spirit will find it hard to get through. We are never entirely disconnected from the spirit world, because we ourselves are spirit, but the spirit world sees our light, not our physical bodies, and negative thoughts will create a fog around that light.

Ultimately, the one thing above all others that will affect how far we progress with our mediumship is our attitude and the way we live our lives. If we learn to interact well with our fellow human beings, it will help us to interact with spirit. We are not aiming to be saints but we need to be there for other people, to allow others to be there for us and to let go of negativity. Negativity of any sort can be harmful and our negative feelings will harm no one but ourselves. Something said by Sharon Harvey a few years ago expressed it very well. "Holding on to hatred," she said "Is like drinking poison and waiting for the other person to die." Jealousy of someone whom we perceive as being a 'better' medium will only diminish our own power.

So, with a sense of commitment, we need to cultivate the belief that we can develop. Without that belief, it won't happen. And, once we start to become confident, we need to keep challenging ourselves. By far and away the best courses I've been on at AFC are those that have challenged me and taken me out of my comfort zone – and I've come home at the end, aware that I've been doing things with my mediumship that I've never done before. We are always capable of more. As Colin Bates has said "If you continually search and ask for something you will eventually get it and it will knock your socks off!" But if we refuse to take on challenges, it means we've settled for second best.

That said, there's a fine line between challenging ourselves to do the best we possibly can and trying for perfection. Perfect mediumship is an impossibility and, by striving for it, we are creating obstacles for ourselves. Because if we're focusing entirely on being right, we'll be scared to be wrong. Not only does this prevent us from giving specific information in case it's not taken but it also means that we will only remember the things we got wrong in a reading (whereas, inevitably, the client will remember all the things we got right). And when we do give a demonstration or a reading that goes particularly well, we'll be additionally nervous the next time because we'll be trying to repeat it, instead of acknowledging that each time is different and all that is required of us is to try our best.

In the many courses I've taken at AFC, I've come to realise that no two mediums work in exactly the same way. And that's as it should be. Our individuality – who we are – is the essence of our mediumship. I suspect that, when we start, we all have a role model, the person who we want to 'be' (I wanted to be Eileen Davies!) – but it'll never happen. We can't be a clone of someone else because we haven't had the life experience of that person, we haven't read all the same books and known all the same people and done all the same things.

So it's important, in our development, to experiment and to find out what works for us, personally. If we go in with rigid ideas of how we want to work, it builds a wall in our auric field and makes it harder for spirit to get through.

PROGRESS

We all develop at different rates, so we need to be patient and to persevere. For me, it took three years before I could be sure of getting a link whenever I stood up to work. Progress comes in fits and starts and you may find yourself on a plateau with no apparent improvement for some time, and then suddenly surge forward. We can't force our development – it happens in spirit's time, not ours. But spirit will never deliberately hold us back – they want us to grow and to become the best we can.

To use an old cliche, mediumship is a journey. But there's no point in focusing on the end of the journey – the ultimate achievement – because there isn't one. Our development is eternal. All we have to do is to immerse ourselves in, and enjoy, every step along the way. As Sharon Harvey has said, we need to allow the magic to happen now. There isn't a road to happiness. The road is happiness. And we don't have to know what's in front of us before taking a step – we just need to trust that the road is there.

But this isn't an easy road – there will be challenges and there will be obstacles. We need both courage and love to overcome them. In a recent trance demonstration by Eileen Davies, one of her guides – an African American woman called Oola – expressed this beautifully. When the road is rocky, she said, "scatter petals of love to soften it under your feet."

Although it may seem at times that you are making no progress, nothing is ever at a complete standstill. It may be that you need to spend time on a particular aspect of your mediumship before moving forward or you may be at a junction where you need to decide which direction you wish to take. It's important not to get frustrated but just to trust to spirit and to carry on working diligently. Never allow negative thoughts to take over. Tell yourself that you can do it, and you will. Don't worry about whether or not you're 'getting it right' – just do it and see what happens. And remember not to compare yourself with other people – they have their stumbling blocks, too, even if you're not aware of them.

It's also important to accept that your mediumship will change constantly. For example, when I first started, spirit attracted my attention through clairaudience. Over time I developed clairvoyance, while clairaudience became less prominent. And, after that, came clairsentience and clairgnosis (where you just know a particular piece of information). Nowadays I get very little clairaudiently but I know that it may well return if spirit thinks it's appropriate.

At times, spirit can be very kind and can give you a foretaste of what is to come in terms of your abilities. Some four years after I started my development, when I was still very much a beginner and lacking in confidence, I was on a course at AFC and was doing a one-to-one with a charming young Dutch man. Suddenly, I was aware of a woman whom I knew, without doubt, was his aunt. I described her easily – the information just flowed – and I got a stream of "yeses". When I'd finished, the young man said to me "You described her perfectly, but I'd have known it was her even if you'd said nothing at all, from your gestures and facial expressions." It was a long time before I got anything close to that again, but the memory of that experience stayed with me and spurred me on. Because, as we're often told at AFC, if you've done it before, you can do it again!

It's important to remember that all mediumship is experimental. We never know what we're going to get. However, our own interests and knowledge can influence the sort of information we receive. When I first started, I was working as a doctor, and spirit would almost invariably give me medical information. Nowadays, I'm a psychotherapist – and I get a lot of information about personality and emotions. Anyone who has ever seen Eileen Davies demonstrate will have been impressed by the number of names – both of people and of places – that she gets. But, on her own admission, she has always found names interesting.

Mediumship is an adventure – we never know what's going to happen until it does. We won't always be brilliant. So much depends on factors such as the energy in the room, the type of communicator that comes through, and the way the audience responds. All we can do is to do our best.

PRACTICE & DEVELOPMENT CIRCLES

I've heard it said that a week at AFC is equivalent to a year sitting in a weekly circle. Whether that's true or not, finding a good circle can be important. However, it's perfectly possible – as long as you are committed to working with and for spirit – to do some development on your own. Tutors can only demonstrate and facilitate – they can't actually teach you how to become a medium. Simone Key often mentions that she started her development by sitting with a friend. Neither had much idea of what they were meant to be doing, but they trusted spirit, and spirit taught them. If you aren't able to find a good circle but you have friends you can work with, just tell spirit what it is you want to do. Remember that we all work differently, so concentrate on understanding how you work with spirit and trust the rest to them.

And certainly, working by yourself is preferable to sitting in a circle where you're not comfortable. A good medium is not necessarily a good teacher. Added to this, not every teacher's methods suit everyone. My personal advice is to find someone who is a good medium, who has integrity and who will both support you and encourage you to become the best you possibly can. You need someone who actively wants to help you to develop and to move on, not someone who wants to keep you in the circle under her guidance for ever. When you find a teacher who gives you what you need, stick with her for as long as you are benefiting from her teaching. And this, I believe, applies to tutors at AFC as well. Over the years I have worked with many of them. When, at the end of a week's course, I go away feeling stimulated and encouraged, knowing that my mediumship has progressed, I know that I will go back to that particular tutor, time and time again.

BASIC EXERCISES FOR DEVELOPMENT

Mind focus exercises for clairvoyance

These exercises will help you not just to focus your mind but also to increase your ability to visualise and to get as much information as possible from images that are given to you by spirit.

1. Pick a colour and a shape, for example a red square. Close your eyes and draw the outline of the shape in your mind. Then colour it in and hold the complete image in your mind for as long as you can. Keep practising until you can hold it for ten minutes.

2. Close your eyes and picture the room you're sitting in. Go round the room, picturing every detail. If your mind strays, start again.

3. Close your eyes and picture the street where you live. Imagine walking down the street and notice every detail of your surroundings as you go.

Self empowerment

1. Make a conscious effort to accept yourself as you are. This doesn't mean that you have to approve your every action (we all do things that we're sorry for later) but that you can accept that you're not perfect, acknowledge your mistakes and learn from them.

2. Remember that every thought creates an action and so, by every thought, we are creating our future. If you think positively you can create positivity. A useful mantra is "I am, I can and I do".

3. Stop thinking "I wish I could" and substitute "I know I can".

4. If you find yourself thinking in a negative way, nip it in the bud as soon as you're aware of it. One way of doing this is to think "cancel, cancel". This is not an easy exercise but it's vital. Negativity will limit your mediumship.

5. Develop an image of yourself full of positivity and power. Feel it. Remember the times when life was really good and recreate the feeling.

6. Appreciate yourself. Write down the things you like about yourself. If you find that hard (and a lot of people do), imagine that you have a friend who is identical to you in all respects. What would you like about that friend?

Manifestation

First, set the intention for what it is you want. Then commit yourself to having the thing that you are manifesting, while being aware of everything (including the negative aspects) that it will bring with it.

Next, visualise your desired outcome in as much detail as you can. After which, make a statement (out loud) about what you are going to achieve, but put it in the present tense. And, finally thank spirit for all that they have helped you to achieve so far.

All you have to do then is to keep going and let go of any thoughts of whether you can do it or how long it's going to take. If you are manifesting to be a great medium, remember that mediumship development is ongoing – there is no end to it.

Facilitation

Spirit will only give you the sort of information that you are familiar with. Eileen Davies believes that the reason she gets a lot of street names is because she has always been interested in these. Reading books of names and their meanings may help you to receive names from spirit. If you're interested in military history, you may get old soldiers coming through to tell you about their military careers. If you're a nurse or a doctor, you are likely to get medical information (when I first started, all I got was medical information!)

So, it's possible to increase the sort of information you receive just by learning more about the world around you.

3

SPIRITUALITY

Do we need to be spiritual to be Spiritualists? The answer to this is, of course, no. One can be a Spiritualist in the same way that one can be a Christian or a Jew or a Muslim, by believing in the tenets of that faith, attending religious services and following a particular code of ethics.

However, when it comes to being a medium, Spiritualism and spirituality are inextricably linked. If we do not work on developing our own spirituality, understanding that we are on an eternal journey of unfoldment, we cannot easily communicate with spirit. We are here on earth to experience life and to move forward in that journey and, in this respect, allowing our spirituality to grow is probably more important than whether we can effectively communicate with the other world.

So what is spirituality? Well, Native American author and theologian, Vine Deloria Jr. (1933-2005) commented that, while religion is for people who're afraid of going to hell, spirituality is for those who've already been there. It is about recognising that we are spiritual beings, developing our relationship with the Divine and allowing it to become a reality in our lives. Spirituality is not fuelled by fear but by understanding and a desire to find the truth of things. And it's this search for the truth that's important, not which road we take to discover it.

Gordon Higginson taught that our job in this lifetime is to spiritualise ourselves. And that's not just about how we relate to the Divine (however we perceive it) but also about how we relate to other living beings. Because how can we form a link to a higher power if we treat our fellow human beings, or animals, badly? Our behaviour is, and must be, an intrinsic part of our spirituality. Someone who declares "I believe in God" but also believes that his or her own religion, nationality or ethnicity is superior to others is not – and cannot be – spiritual. Because the message of all great spiritual leaders and teachers is not just about the power of belief in the Divine but is also about the power of love.

In order to develop our spirituality, we need to to trust that spirit will always be there for us and will always guide us. The mystical poet William Blake wrote:

If the Sun and Moon should doubt
They'd immediately go out

Good mediumship is fuelled by love and compassion. The 18th century philosopher and mystic Emanuel Swedenborg described love as being food for the spiritual body. So, as mediums we need to demonstrate our trust and to try to live our lives in love and truth and in a way that can be an example that others will want to follow.

Being an example to others, however, doesn't mean we have to be perfect. Striving for perfection is pointless because true perfection is impossible. But we can still be inspirational in the way that we deal with and try to overcome our imperfections. A determination to hold ourselves to a high standard in all things and a constant awareness of our interaction with others is all that is necessary. The 19th century poet Francis Thompson put this concept into verse:

Spirituality

All things by immortal power,
Near or far,
Hiddenly
To each other linked are,
That thou canst not stir a flower
Without troubling of a star.

4

WORKING WITH GUIDES

WHO ARE OUR GUIDES?

Spirit guides are often depicted as Native Americans, or Tibetan lamas or Chinese philosophers. But the truth is that they can manifest in numerous ways.

Some years ago, I asked – just as I was going to sleep – to be given the name of my guide. That night, I dreamed that I was in a Middle Eastern bazaar. On one stall there was a large mirror and, looking into it, I saw a face that was not my own but that of an ancient Egyptian woman – like those you see in the murals that have been found in Egyptian tombs. Shortly after this I woke up and heard a voice – outside my head but close to my ear – saying "Agabori". Later that day, I Googled the name and found it was a word from a north African dialect meaning "that's beautiful".

However, we don't have just one guide each. And, while it's great to know the name of one or more of our guides (because, after all, it's the usual thing to know the names of people who you work closely with) you don't actually need to know them. Indeed, a guide is not a person as we understand the term but, rather, a pure light energy which only takes on a name and an appearance for the benefit of those with whom it is communicating.

Probably one of the best known guides is Silver Birch who, through the trance medium Maurice Barbanell, offered wisdom and spiritual insight over a period of years in the mid 20th century. He has been portrayed by a spirit artist as a Native American and that is what those who heard him speak took him to be. However, the website of the Spiritual Truth Foundation which now holds the copyright to these teachings tells us that "There is evidence to suggest that this was simply a convenient persona behind which a far more spiritually evolved soul hid in order that those who read his words would judge them not by the name attached to them but by the wisdom that pervades every sentence."

Sometimes people say that they have family members – their grandmother, for example – as guides. However, according to Simone Key, this isn't correct as our guides can't be emotionally attached to us. Which is not to say that our family members can't be around us and looking after us – but they are helpers, not guides.

Our guides are with us at our birth and stay with us throughout our lives. However, different guides with different roles may be predominant at different times in our development. As we advance and our knowledge grows, so the appropriate guides will be there to help us.

HOW WE WORK WITH OUR GUIDES

Most tutors stress the importance of learning to recognise the energy of our guides. We don't have to know their names or what they look like but just have to trust that if we need them to be there, they will be. A useful exercise is to sit quietly and invite your guides to come close and to give you some indication of their closeness. Then ask them to step back. And then invite them to come close again. Be aware of what you feel. For me, it's a gentle pressure on the left side of my head. Common experiences include a feeling of 'cobwebs' across your face, a tickling sensation or just an awareness of a change in the energy, as would happen if someone came over to stand behind you.

Each guide has a different role so, for example, the guide who works with us when we are giving healing will not be the same guide who helps us with our mediumship. We just need to trust them to give us the help that is appropriate to the moment. Some tutors say that we can have up to a hundred guides.

WHAT IS THE ROLE OF THE GUIDE?

Our guides are not omniscient or omnipotent. The last of the Seven Principles of Spiritualism is "Eternal progress open to every human soul". Spiritualists believe that the journey is unending and, ultimately, will reach levels of development that, in our present human state, we cannot even begin to imagine. It follows, therefore, that all the souls and energies in the world of spirit are developing and progressing as well – and that includes our guides. They, too, are on a journey of discovery.

In terms of the work we do in mediumship, our guides are the mediators or facilitators who help individual spirit people to come through or who help to focus the energy of healing. And, of course, the guides of mediums who work in trance will offer teaching and philosophy. But it's not just in these situations that they are present. They are with us at all times, and can even work with us in our sleep.

When giving a spirit communication, Matthew Smith says that all you have to do is open your mind and then open your mouth. And if you get in a muddle, ask your guides to help you to sort it out. For example, if you get some evidence that feels right but your recipient can't take it, ask for it to be given to you in a different way (as it's probably your interpretation that's wrong rather than the information itself).

Speak to your guides, as you would to a friend, and ask them to show you how you can best work with them. They are called guides for a reason!

5

MEDITATION AND SITTING IN THE POWER

WHAT IS MEDITATION?

This first section is not taken from teachings by AFC tutors. However, I have included it because I believe it is helpful to understand the different forms that meditation can take, and how it differs from sitting in the power.

Dictionary Definitions

Dictionary definitions of meditation include:

- giving your attention to only one thing, either as a religious activity or as a way of becoming calm and relaxed
- the act of remaining in a silent and calm state for a period of time
- engaging in mental exercise for the purpose of reaching a heightened level of spiritual awareness

All of which is somewhat confusing until you realise that meditation is not a single type of practice but a generic term used to describe a wide range of different, and mainly religious, practices.

Tranquility Meditation

This is extensively practised by followers of Buddhism who distinguish between *samatha* ('tranquility' or 'concentration') meditation and *vipassana* ('insight') meditation.

Perhaps the simplest form of tranquility meditation is that of concentrating on the breath as it goes in and out. (By 'simple', I don't mean easy – anyone who has tried this knows how difficult it is to maintain without the mind going off in all directions!). The Buddhist practice *anapanasati* (mindfulness of breathing) and the Taoist practice *zhuanqi* are examples of this.

I remember the great Rinzai Zen teacher, the Venerable Mykyo-ni (1921-2007), with whom I had the privilege of studying, explaining the basic practice: you breathe in and then, on the out breath, you count 'one', you breathe in and then, on the out breath, you count 'two', and when you reach ten, or if you lose your concentration, you start again at one. "So," she said "the way it goes is this: one . . . two . . . I wonder what to have for supper . . . one . . . two . . . I must remember to 'phone Susan . . . one . . . two . . . BORING!" Which is exactly what most of us experience when starting out with this type of meditation. However, if you can learn, in Myokyo-ni's words, to "give yourself into the practice", and to practise regularly, it becomes easier over time.

Other forms of tranquility meditation include Buddhist walking meditation, Hindu *tattva* meditation (where the mind is focused on a particular chakra and an associated symbol), the Soto Zen practice of 'just sitting' (described on the website of the Soto Zen Buddhist Association as "being oneself, with nothing extra, in harmony with the way things are") and the Taoist *zuowang* in which the aim is to empty the mind completely.

But how do you empty the mind? It's the nature of the mind to have chatter and ideas running through it. We need to learn the skill of letting go. I remember another Buddhist teacher, Alf Vial, saying "If you're sitting in meditation and a sausage swims into your mind, just acknowledge it and let it go because, if you hang on to it, before you know where you are, you'll have a mixed grill!"

Emptying the mind is a skill that can be valuable to mediums because, the more we can clear our minds of our own thoughts, the more easily we can receive what spirit is trying to tell us.

There is one situation, however, when a tranquility meditation is not likely to be helpful – and that's just before we do a spirit communication. Evidential mediumship requires an active mind, which is why, very often in a church, some bright cheerful music will be played before a medium stands up to demonstrate, in order to raise the energy level.

Insight Meditation

The Sri Lankan Buddhist monk Bhante Henepola Gunaratana has described *vipassana* meditation as a practice in which "the meditator uses his concentration as a tool by which his awareness can chip away at the wall of illusion that cuts him off from the living light of reality".

In Rinzai Zen, insight meditation involves the practitioner concentrating on a *koan*, a paradoxical statement or question (such as "what is the sound of one hand clapping?") which, ultimately, may bring him to a higher understanding of reality.

Mantra Meditation

This form of meditation is common in Hindu practice but is also found in Tibetan Buddhism and in Sufism. A mantra is a word or phrase that is repeated over and over again, with both the meaning of the word and the sound of it being used to create an altered state of awareness. Transcendental meditation, which became very popular in the 1960s and 1970s, when it was espoused by the Beatles, is a form of mantra meditation.

Some people and sects have used specific mantras to try to manifest wealth or other personal benefits.

Meditation With a Specific Aim

An example of this is the Buddhist practice of *mettabhavana* (development of loving-kindness) in which practitioners send love first to themselves, then to their nearest and dearest, then their acquaintances, and so on, outwards, until love is being sent to the whole population – human and animal – of the world. As I mentioned in Chapter Two, this can be a valuable practice for self-development.

Another practice with a specific aim is the yoga *kundalini* meditation, which concentrates on awakening the *kundalini* energy, said to lie dormant at the base of the spine.

Visualisation

In effect, visualisation meditation is very similar to a daydream and takes the meditators into the same state, where they become caught up in what is happening in their minds and less aware of the real world. It is used extensively by hypnotherapists both to induce a hypnotic trance and to deepen a trance.

Like daydreams, it can take many forms. A quite popular one is where the participants are asked to picture themselves walking through a wood until they come to a clearing with a large log in the centre, on which they sit. Someone (a 'wise person' or a loved one in spirit) then comes out of the trees, sits on the log and has a conversation with the meditator. While the meditation leader describes the walk through the woods in detail, nothing more is said after the meditator has been joined by the second person, until it's time to come out of the meditation. It can therefore be seen as a mixture of both tranquility meditation and insight meditation since, sometimes, the wisdom coming from the person who is met in the clearing can be quite profound.

Leah Bond took us through a beautiful visualisation at a recent course at AFC. You start by focusing on your base chakra and choosing a shade of red that's right for you on that day. Then allow the red to flow out into your aura. Once you've done that, focus on the sacral chakra and do the same with the colour orange. Then the solar plexus chakra and yellow, the heart chakra and green, the throat chakra and blue, the brow chakra and indigo, and finally the crown chakra and violet. When all these colours have flowed out into your aura, creating a wonderful rainbow, visualise the silver cord that attaches you to the spirit world and allow it to become stronger.

THE ROLE OF MEDITATION IN THE DEVELOPMENT OF MEDIUMSHIP

Concentration and focus are vital to good mediumship. Meditation can help this by training us to let go of ego and focus solely on the spark of divinity that is within each of us. Tony Stockwell has said that through meditation we can become a greater manifestation of what we are meant to be. Eileen Davies teaches that meditation harmonises the right and left brain (the emotional/creative side and the logical side) and nourishes and develops our auric field. This last effect is very important because it is the light of our auras that attracts the spirit world to us.

I was fortunate enough to hear an excellent talk on meditation given at AFC by Kitty Woud in which she emphasised the value of the practice in allowing us to discover who we really are. In addition, meditation helps to discipline the mind – something that is essential for mediumship. It dissolves the barriers between us and God, us and spirit, and us and other people, as well as sensitising our psychic faculties. And while we practise, energy builds and fills the reservoir of the auric field – something that also happens when we sit in the power.

SITTING IN THE POWER

Although this is sometimes referred to as meditation it is quite different from the various methods described above. It is, perhaps, closest to the Christian practice of "sitting with God" or the Sufi practice of *muraqabah* ('the contemplation of God'). In other words, while other forms of meditation can be used as a self development or relaxation practice, sitting in the power is necessarily a spiritual practice.

Andrew Manship has described it as "sitting in the light of your being". In order to connect with the light of the spirit world we have to recognise and grow our own light. Only thus can we blend with spirit. There is a similarity with the Tibetan Buddhist concept of "self power, other power". Development cannot be one-sided. If we want spirit to work with us, we need to develop in such a way that we can blend with ease. And here the similarity to the Buddhist concept becomes stronger because, once that link or blending has occurred, we become aware that there is, in fact, no 'self' and no 'other'. We are all spirit.

But what is the power? How can we recognise it? The answers to these questions are things we have to find out for ourselves by investigation and practice. We need to understand how the power touches us and how we respond to it. In earlier times, many of the great mediums spent months or years learning to become at one with the power before they ever started to do spirit communications. It's also important to remember that this is a personal journey – no two people experience or embrace the power in the same way but, for each of us, spirit will support us in every step along the way.

WORKING IN THE POWER

The reason why practising sitting in the power is so important is because we can only link with the power of spirit when we are in contact with our own power. Martin Twycross (teaching on SNUi, the online branch of the Spiritualists' National Union) has observed that to work without building power is like trying to drive a car without petrol. However, this doesn't mean that we need to be in a state of power all the time. We need to learn how to go into the power, maintain it while we're working and then let go of it when we have finished.

If you're truly in the power, your senses will become heightened and you will lose some of your sense of self. You will be aware of the presence of spirit and the words you need will just come to you.

The main difficulty that most people face is staying in the power when they are working. It happens especially with people who are just starting their journey of mediumship. They link in quite successfully and the contact is accepted by the sitter. However, it then seems to get harder and the medium may feel that the spirit communicator has stepped back. But actually what has happened is that the medium has allowed the power to drop and has lost the connection. Very often this occurs after the recipient has been unable to take a particular piece of information – which is why tutors put such emphasis on what to do when the sitter says "no". (This will be covered in a later chapter.) Silence on the part of the medium can also cause a drop in the power which is why you will hear tutors say "keep talking".

Maintaining the power is something that only comes with practice and this is why it's important not to start demonstrating publicly before you're ready. Once you're secure in getting a connection you should be able to hold the power for one link or even two. But working in a church or offering an 'evening of mediumship' means you need to be able to work for anything between thirty minutes and two hours. And your last links need to be just as good as your first.

TECHNIQUES

When you sit in the power, you are linking to your guides, so it's quite possible to do this as an exercise on its own, without bringing in spirit communicators. It can help to start with a little mantra such as that suggested by Sandie Baker: "As I move my mind to the power of spirit, I wish to serve."

There are many techniques that can help us move into the power. It's important to find the way that works best for you personally. These are some of the techniques that I have been taught at AFC and in the online tuition programme run by the SNUi (Spiritualists' National Union international). With all of them, you first have to find the power – the divine light – within yourself and then build it up in order to link with spirit.

1. Starting With the Chakras

Look within yourself and locate the chakra that is the centre of your being. You may feel instinctively that it is your heart chakra – but look carefully, it may equally be the solar plexus, the throat, the brow or even the crown chakra. Then focus on the power and the light within that chakra and allow it to build up.

2. Draw the Power Up

Imagine that there is a pillow of light under your feet. Feel it pressing upwards. Draw the light up through your feet and push it right up through your entire body.

Or be aware of all the energy surrounding you and then draw power up through your feet and down through your crown chakra. Keep focused on the power – listen to the energy.

3. Visualise the Power

Imagine a column of white light. Breathe it in and draw it up through your feet. When you are filled with light, allow yourself to become part of the column.

4. Visualising the Power as a Colour

Think of the power as a colour and, in your imagination, place it at the base of your spine. Draw it up your spine to the second (sacral) chakra. Count to three, then let it sink down again. Then repeat this, drawing it up to the third (solar plexus) chakra, and so on.

5. Visualising a Candle Flame

Think of a candle flame and, once it is fixed in your mind, bring it inside you. Then slowly expand it.

Or imagine a glow in your base chakra and allow it to grow into a flame.

In either case, with each in-breath, allow the light to expand so that it fills your body, then the room you're sitting in and then the whole building, after which allow it to grow still more and flood out into the world.

6. Methods Devised by Students at AFC

The only difference between us and spirit is that we have physical bodies. However, the spiritual – or energetic – part of us is almost identical. Focus on the light within you and imagine it expanding outwards to merge with the spiritual energies surrounding it.

Or see your power opening up like a peacock's tail all around you.

Or imagine you have a foot-pump (such as you'd use to blow up a bicycle tyre) and picture yourself pumping power through your body and expanding it outwards.

Remember that, whichever technique you choose, it is important to begin from a position of love – for yourself and for spirit. Then invite spirit to draw near. You need to make clear your intention – tell the other world that you are there for them and they will be drawn to the love that you are sending out.

Ideally you should sit in the same place each time, because it will retain some of the power so that every time you sit it will become stronger. If you don't have a whole room that you can dedicate to your mediumship, sit in the corner of a room where the energy is less likely to be disturbed by other activities. Opinions differ as to how long you need to sit each day - but most tutors say somewhere between five and twenty minutes. This makes it fairly achievable even for those people who lead very busy lives.

Kitty Woud recommends that we experiment to see what works best for us – sitting in the power, meditation or both.

6

THE MECHANICS
OF MEDIUMSHIP

Before we get onto the actual techniques of mediumship, it may be helpful to look at what is actually happening when we work psychically and with spirit.

Perhaps the most important thing is to remember that we, too, are spirit. And, when we work, we are working spirit to spirit, whether it is psychically with the spirit of our sitter or mediumistically with a discarnate spirit.

But how are we doing that? As we are incarnate rather than discarnate, everything has to be channelled through the brain. And, while there's still a lot that scientists don't know about how the brain works, an electroencephalogram or EEG is able to show various patterns of electrical impulses or brain waves that indicate different states of consciousness.

- Beta waves are associated with a fully conscious state in which all five senses are functioning.

- Alpha waves show that we have moved into the subconscious in which we tend to lose sense of time and can work with our intuition, clairvoyance, clairaudience, clairsentience and clairgnosis ('just knowing'). This is the state that, ideally, we should stay in when we are doing a spirit communication. However, it is all too easy to slip back into the beta state if we start to query or interpret the information that is being given to us.

- Theta waves indicate that we are in the superconscious state, in which mental mediumship has greater power and greater energy.

- Delta waves are the sign of a profoundly altered state in which there is a link with the universal consciousness. Physical mediums work at this level, as do some trance mediums, although trance can also operate at the theta level.

While it is interesting to look at the scientific description of what goes on in a medium's brain, there is more to it than just a change in the electrical impulses. Vitally important to our ability to communicate with spirit is our attitude. I have already mentioned, in Chapter Two, Eileen Davies' assertion that everything we do comes from a place of love or a place of fear. I remember her illustrating this beautifully with a little experiment using applied kinesiology. She asked one of the students to stand with her arm stretched out to the side and to resist while another student tried to push the arm down. The subject resisted fairly easily. Then Eileen put a card on which something was written into the first student's hand. This time, the arm was pushed down easily. The student was given a different card and now was able to resist very strongly. Eileen then revealed what had been written on the cards – on the first was the word 'fear' and on the second was the word 'love'.

Love strengthens a communication. Approaching mediumistic work with love for spirit and love for the recipient will greatly facilitate your work. Approaching it with fear or anxiety will hinder it. This was brought home to me on one occasion when I was on a weekend course led by Eileen Davies. Something had happened to me during the previous week which had distressed me deeply and had caused my self confidence to plummet and, as a result, I wasn't really in the right place for working mediumistically. Eileen asked me to stand up in front of the class and demonstrate and I said I'd rather not (most unusual for me). However, I was persuaded to do so. But once there, nothing came. My mind was blank and I was close to tears. Until Eileen said to me "Just remember that there's someone in the world of spirit who really wants to speak to someone here who is longing to hear from them." My heart went out to both spirit and recipient as I felt their need, and the situation was no longer about my fear. Immediately I was aware of a communicator and I went on to give a good demonstration.

WORKING PSYCHICALLY

Our bodily and mental health affect our aura which is why we can tell if someone is stressed or angry or depressed, even if they're trying hard to disguise it. We sense it rather than seeing it. The energy from their aura is sending messages to ours.

Plenty of experiments have been done that seem to show that plants grow better if we talk to them and make a fuss of them. And the experiments of the Japanese writer and researcher Masaru Emoto seem to show that ice crystals are more likely to distort if the water from which they form is subjected first to negative energies such as anger.

Similarly, ill health, because it affects our auras, may affect our psychic and mediumistic abilities – for better or for worse. I remember, a number of years ago, meeting a lady who, having been a working medium for much of her life, found that she could no longer make a good link after suffering a small stroke. However, I have also met someone whose mediumistic abilities were greatly enhanced after she had a stroke. But why in some cases the effect is beneficial and in others detrimental I have been unable to discover.

WORKING MEDIUMISTICALLY

Mediumship works through the nervous system, with the brain converting the energies that spirit sends us into pictures, sounds, feelings, tastes and smells. Communication with spirit is, in effect, a form of telepathy – the mind of the spirit sending messages directly to our mind.

By sending out love and making clear our intention to connect, we increase the light in our auric fields, and this is what spirit sees and is drawn to. By believing that it will happen, we are giving power to the connection.

We constantly talk about how difficult good mediumship can be to achieve – but tutors at AFC often remind us that it is not easy for spirit, either. They, too, require power to communicate with us. And this is why information will often be succinct, rather than spelled out in full. Sometimes information will be given in the form of symbols or colours. We will *feel* that something is right or will just *know* it. Feeling, says Eileen Davies, is the language of spirit.

If we are very fortunate, we will develop clairaudience. This is a real gift because, if we are truly hearing the words that spirit is saying, we are not going to get it wrong. In addition, hearing someone's voice can tell you more about the speaker – where he comes from, his level of education, even his age group and his personality. But true clairaudience is uncommon. Eileen Davies believes that this is because we are saturated with noise in our everyday lives and so have densensitised ourselves to sound.

ALTERED STATES

All mediumship entails being in an altered state – as shown by the change from beta brain waves to alpha, theta or delta. All this means, in terms of spirit communication, is that you will be engrossed in your work, the information will flow freely and, when you have finished, you might not remember everything that you have said.

People who come new to mediumship may sometimes be concerned about how close the link is with spirit during this altered state, particularly with reference to trance. It is important to understand that spirit will never enter or 'possess' your body. It will simply enter your aura, in the same way that, when you shake hands with someone or hug them, your energies and theirs will inevitably contact each other.

Spirit will only come if we ask them to. If we constantly hear or see spirit, or if information keeps coming into our minds when we're not working, it's because we are allowing it to. If this happens to you, all you have to do is to ask spirit to step back. Tell them when you will next be working (in circle or demonstration) and ask them to return then.

Similarly, some people complain that, when they are about to fall asleep at night and are in that altered state between waking and sleeping, they keep seeing faces. As Simone Key points out, it's not spirit coming to annoy you – it's you moving out towards them.

The answer to all these problems is good personal discipline, helped by regular sitting in the power, so that you can learn how to move in and, just as importantly, move out again.

7

PREPARING TO WORK WITH SPIRIT

APPROACHING MEDIUMSHIP IN THE RIGHT WAY

In Chapter Two we looked at the importance of having the right attitude when starting out on the path of spiritual and mediumistic development. That attitude becomes even more important when we start to make contact with spirit.

Trust is essential – both in ourselves and in spirit. If we believe that we can't do something, the chances are that we are correct. But the reason our belief is correct – the reason we can't do whatever it is – is simply because we don't believe that we can. We are limiting our abilities by our own beliefs. This is true in many of life's situations, but particularly so with mediumship. Because if we say, for example, "I can't get names", spirit will hear us and won't give us names because we're not open to them. On the other hand, if we say "I'm not yet able to get names right every time", we are telling ourselves – and spirit – that we can get names and, while we may not always get them right at the moment, we believe we can do that that some time in the future. Which is fine.

The same attitude applies to ways of working. If we say "I'm clairvoyant" or "I'm not clairaudient" we're limiting ourselves in terms of our future development. Think of all the things you do now – perhaps you're a parent, or you drive a car, or you're a teacher or a nurse or an electrician. When you were five years old you were none of these things. You had to develop into them. And with spiritual and mediumistic development we don't just have a lifetime to develop them – we have an eternity. Remember that the seventh principle of the SNU is "Eternal progress open to every human soul" – and that there is no such thing as a fully developed medium.

There have been reports in the newspapers over the years of people exhibiting super-human strength just because they didn't stop to think about what they were doing – for example, a mother lifting a car because her child was trapped underneath it. I've seen Jose Medrado get four people to lift a man out of a chair, using just their forefingers and middle fingers, because a little ritual done beforehand allowed them to believe that they could do it. Such feats lead us to wonder how much more we could do if only we believed that we could.

Of course, for many of the things we achieve in life, while belief in ourselves is a good place to start, commitment, hard work and a great deal of learning are also essential. And it's no different for mediumship. But it's important to remember that learning to get it right means that, sometimes, you have to get it wrong. If nothing ever went wrong, how would we progress? A handout I received from Eileen Davies on a recent course at AFC had the following statement: "There are no mistakes, for every experience is a positive opportunity to learn a valuable lesson which will aid you in your progression."

There's a story (probably apocryphal) about Thomas Edison and his invention of the light bulb. He knew in his heart of hearts that such a thing was possible – he just didn't know how. So he experimented. And on the two thousandth attempt, it worked. But someone said to him "That must have been dreadful, having all those attempts that failed." To which Edison's reply was "They didn't fail. They just showed me another way which didn't work."

In our mediumship, we will continually find ways that don't work for us. So it's important to remember that we all work differently. We have to find our own way of working, rather than try slavishly to copy someone else. I saw a sign the other day that said "Be yourself. An original is always worth more than a copy."

Ultimately, though, it is spirit who will determine how we're going to work – whether we will be healers or demonstrators or trance mediums. So we need to go into the work with no expectations but simply with the intention of going wherever spirit takes us.

Finally, remember that even the great mediums don't get it right all the time. But the difference between them and the rest of us is that they aren't afraid of getting it wrong.

INCORPORATING MEDIUMSHIP INTO YOUR LIFE

Mediumship should not just be something that we do. It should be who we are. Although your team of guides and helpers won't desert you or give up on you if you don't make contact with them for a few weeks, or even months, you will find that you work much better if you are in contact with them regularly. Open your mind to spirit for a few minutes every day, let them know that you want to work with them and that you trust them to take you along the path that is right for you. Build a relationship with them and get to know them.

Allow spirit to help you to develop love, understanding, compassion and patience in your life. And although there may be times when you feel like giving up, know that spirit never will but will always be there to help you through the difficult times as well as the good ones.

8

USING YOUR MEDIUMSHIP:

Protection – Linking – Staying in the Power – Placing the Contact

You may feel that a lot of this chapter, and of the following three, is about demonstrating but most of what's said applies to private readings as well. Getting in the power, making a link, getting accurate evidence and using the right vocabulary should be the same, no matter how you are working.

And, while Chapter Eleven is mostly to do with demonstrating in public, it applies just as much to demonstrating in a group at AFC or in your circle at home.

PROTECTION

Newcomers to mediumship often ask about the need for protection. And, indeed, I have met the occasional student who has been so concerned about what opening up might attract that she has been in the habit of spending ten or fifteen minutes – or even more – performing elaborate protection rituals before starting to connect with spirit. But any tutor at AFC will tell you that this is completely unnecessary.

When you open up to spirit, you are allowing your inner light to shine and grow. It is this light that attracts spirit to you. And it is also this light that protects you. As Matthew Smith has said, the only thing you need to protect yourself from is ignorance.

MAKING A LINK

Before you can make a link, you have to be in the power. Getting into, and sitting in, the power was covered in Chapter Five. When someone is just starting out in mediumship, getting into the power may be quite difficult, but links can still be made. However, without being fully in the power, it is well-nigh impossible to sustain a link for more than a minute or two and the information that is received is likely to be patchy and quite superficial. This is why sitting in the power, even for just a few minutes a day, can make such a difference to your mediumship.

I have mentioned elsewhere in this book that it was three years before I could be confident of getting a link. It was, for me, a very hit or miss affair, mainly because I was never quite sure how to do it. I am permanently indebted to Sharon Harvey who, in a workshop one afternoon at AFC, told us that making a link "is only a thought". Since then, I've heard other tutors say it in other ways. Simone Key tells us to express our intention – we tell spirit that we intend to link and it happens. Matthew Smith teaches that "The other world is only a thought away. All we have to do is ask for their help." And Gordon Higginson used to tell his students to "Simply ask who's there".

You can make your life easier (and your evidence better) by asking for someone to come through who was well known to the recipient (so as to be easily recognised), who had a strong personality (so you can feel it more readily) and who is a good communicator (so you will get plenty of information). Let spirit know that this is always the sort of communicator you would like when you work. You can also try asking for a man, a woman or a child or someone in a specific age group, although my own feeling is that spirit may not always want to comply with this. There may be someone who wants to come through urgently and, if they're not the gender or age that you've asked for, their arrival could confuse you. In addition to which, learning to distinguish the gender and assess the age of the communicator is one of the basic skills of mediumship.

There are three common problems that can prevent us from making a link – one is anxiety about performing, the second is not believing that we can and the third is trying too hard. If one of these is something that affects you, try to relax – remind yourself that you're just practising and, in the grand scheme of things, it doesn't really matter whether you get a link on this particular occasion. Then think back to those occasions when you did get a good link, because success feeds success. Remember, too, that the spirit world is always there (where else would it be?) and will never leave you standing on a platform or in a circle without a communicator. If you believe that someone is there, he or she will be.

However, if you are still nervous about getting a link, there are various visualisations that can make it easier:

- Imagine that there is a golden mist, a waterfall or a beautiful silk curtain behind you and ask spirit to step through it and join you

- Imagine a high backed chair. There is someone sitting in it but you can only see their hands. Describe the person those hands belong to. (It's amazing what you can tell about someone just from looking at their hands).

- Imagine a page with handwriting on it. Describe the person who wrote it.

- Get an image of an animal that symbolises the person who is coming through and use that to get into the description (for example, a dove might tell you that the person was quiet and gentle and rather shy, while a horse might tell you that he was strong, athletic and determined – or however you perceive the particular animal).

But remember that there is no right or wrong way of making a link – we all have to find what suits us individually. The important thing – whichever way we do it – is to relax the mind and focus on the other world. Mediumship works best when we have no preconceived ideas about what is going to happen. As Eileen Davies reminds us, the great pioneers of spiritualism had no one to tell them what they were likely to experience.

As soon as you are aware of spirit, start talking. Say the first thing that comes into your head. Allow the information to flow.

It's important to remember that, while you need to build your power before you get your link, you should avoid making a link before you stand up. If you get information before you're ready to give it, your mind can start to embellish it and interpret it and, even if you're able to hold the information in your head without doing this, it will not sound as vibrant and alive to your audience as it will do if you are getting the information through as you speak. And, of course, you'll need to make sure you hold on to the link so that you can continue the communication when you do stand up.

STAYING IN THE POWER

Staying in the power is essential for consistent mediumship. Not only does a demonstration in a church or at an 'evening of mediumship' require you to stay in the power for anything between 30 minutes and two hours, but the more energy you have, the better your evidence will be.

If you practise sitting in the power regularly, moving into the power – and being the power – will become second nature. And once you are in that space, information will flow readily. If you focus on the power, the message will take care of itself.

When we contact the spirit world, they're not coming in to us – we are going out to them. So it's up to us and not them to ensure the closeness necessary for a good communication. The ideal is to lose yourself in the power so you start to become the power itself.

At the start of your demonstration, pull up the power (which you will have been building for some time beforehand) and mentally throw it over the audience. Or visualise it as light and fill the whole room with it. Gordon Higginson was a master of manipulating power. At the start of a demonstration (and he demonstrated in some huge halls) he would project the power right to the back of the room and his first contacts would be for recipients at the back. Then, as he worked progressively further forward in the hall, he would allow the power to start to roll back towards him.

In a demonstration, you're working with the combined energy of everyone present, but sometimes this can be quite sluggish. If energy is lacking in the room, mentally ask spirit to help you, and fill the place with love. Your own power can then compensate for what is lacking in the audience.

It helps to send a request out to spirit for the first contact to be for someone at the back of the room. Work within the energy and, when it lessens over time, ask spirit for recipients nearer the front. And, for each contact, when you have found your recipient throw your energy over him or her so that you, spirit and recipient are energetically linked.

Unfortunately, it's all too easy to let the power drop during a demonstration, but there are things you can do to avoid this. The first of these is to keep talking – if you pause in your delivery, your energy will drop and there is a risk that your mind will take over. Avoid closing your eyes as this, too, can cause a drop in energy. Build a rapport with the audience and, if you can, make them laugh.

Another way to maintain energy is to ensure that you don't look down. There is a tendency, especially among mediums who are just beginning their training, to look down at their feet if the information isn't flowing well, or if the recipient says "no" to something. So, in effect, they are letting the power drop at exactly the moment when they need it most. Training yourself to lift your head or to focus on a spot at the back of the room will help you to maintain your energy.

It's also important not to query what you're getting. If you say something along the lines of "I'm seeing such-and-such – but I don't know why", it means that you don't have faith in yourself and, as a result, both your energy and that of the audience will drop. Simone Key advises students to "Believe you're the best medium in the world."

Moving around the platform or moving your hands as you speak can also help to maintain the energy. However, you should ensure that you're not moving excessively (which could well distract your audience from what you are saying) and that you're not performing one movement, or set of movements, over and over again. Mesmerising the audience by allowing them to focus on your step forward – step left – step back – step right routine will make it hard for any of them to listen to your words.

And, in a demonstration, it's important to get the audience to contribute to the energy (whether they realise they are doing it or not). Try to engage them by making everyone feel a part of what is going on, and by asking those who receive messages to speak up clearly. Once a recipient begins to say "yes" in response to the evidence, it will raise the energy as other people start to hope that you will go to them with the next contact. It's important, though, to ensure that you're with the correct person – if you're not, the energy will drop.

Another thing that can affect the energy is if you ask spirit too many questions. By all means, send a thought about the sort of information you would like, but if you go searching for specific information (such as their age when they died or what they died from) it can cause the energy to drop because it may be something that they don't want to tell you and because it takes your concentration away from what they are trying to say.

If, despite following all these guidelines, you still feel your energy dropping, don't panic! Have a sip of water and just take a few seconds to rebuild your power.

And, at the end of the demonstration or reading, don't forget to shut down. As mediums, we can't afford to be open all the time – it's not good for our health and it's not good for our work.

PLACING THE CONTACT

Once you're aware of the communicator, you need to find the recipient as quickly as possible. There are different views on how to place the contact. Some people go directly to the recipient, others throw out the first few pieces of information and then ask who can take it.

There are, it has to be said, drawbacks to the first method. First of all, if you go directly, you need to make sure that the evidence you have is detailed and specific, and not generic. If you say "I have a lady who was a grandmother, had grey hair, wore glasses and passed in her eighties . . . I believe I'm with the lady in red.", half the people in the audience will be thinking "Has the medium gone to the right person? It sounds just like my grandmother."

Another drawback is that, if you go direct, the sense of expectation and of "is this going to be for me" is reduced in the audience as a whole, and the energy will drop.

A third drawback is that, while you may feel drawn to someone in the audience, it may just be their spiritual light that's attracting you, rather than the fact that they're the true recipient. And if you go direct to the wrong person, you're really in trouble. Getting something as basic as the identity of the recipient wrong can lead the audience to wonder how accurate the rest of your information is, and you'll lose credibility.

In addition, if you go direct, some people will believe you are working psychically, not mediumistically, especially if your evidence is at all vague.

If you throw information out, on the other hand, you can't afford to be vague – otherwise you'll get half the audience putting their hands up and it will take you all day to sort them out. So throwing it out is much better practice because you simply have to be specific and get good evidence. Ideally, you should give about four or five pieces of information, then ask "Who am I with?" and see no more than two or three hands go up.

All the tutors I've worked with at AFC use the 'throw it out method'. But some, after the first few pieces of information, will go to one area of the room (for example, "I feel I'm at the back on the left hand side") and may then go directly to one person in that area. However, on a couple of occasions I've seen a tutor, demonstrating in the Sanctuary at AFC, get this wrong – which just goes to show how very difficult it can be! And when it does turn out not to be with that person – particularly if a fair amount of evidence has already been given and accepted – it can leave her feeling very disappointed that the message isn't for her, after all.

It is probably safest, therefore, to ensure that you get really specific information, throw it out (perhaps with a general indication of where you feel you are) and let the recipient self-select. But even this isn't problem-free because here you run the risk of falling prey to a message-grabber. There are some people, unfortunately, who are so desperate for a message that they're itching to put their hands up as soon as you've said "I have a lady who is a grandmother". So, while you may opt for recipient self-selection, it's still vital to know whether you're with the right person. Matthew Smith calls this the 'magnetic pull'. And, indeed, the energy feels quite different when you are with the right person, so learning to recognise this is important. If you're finding that the information isn't flowing easily, you can be pretty sure that you're with the wrong person.

The ultimate test, of course, is to check with the communicator. This is important because, sometimes, a spirit may come through who is very similar to a friend or relative of someone in the audience who is not connected to them. Simone Key tells the story of bringing through a young man who wanted to speak to his parents and having all the information accepted by a couple at the front of the hall. There was no question of them being message grabbers – they could genuinely accept all the information. But then the communicator said to Simone "I don't know these people." In the end, the recipients were identified further back in the hall – but they hadn't put their hands up earlier because the first couple seemed so sure that it was for them.

If you find you've gone to the wrong person, it's important to tell them so – apologetically – as soon as you're aware that the message isn't for them. If you've fallen foul of a message grabber, you might want to add that you'll try to come back to her later (which recognises her need and sends the thought out to spirit that this person would really like a message).

If no one can take the initial information think back briefly to what you've said and decide which pieces you're really sure about. Repeat them and ask if anyone can take those. Or ask "Who can take most of the information?" Never ask "Who can take any of the information?" or three quarters of the room will put a hand up (particularly if you've said this was a grandparent!). If someone says he or she can take some of it, ask "What can you take?" not "What can't you take?" as the latter will distract you (and the audience) from what you've got right and may cause the energy to drop.

The amount of information you give right at the start needs to be just right, too. If you give too little, you are likely to get a large number of people who can take it. But, if you give too much, those people in the audience who definitely can't take the information will lose interest and the energy will drop. In addition, if the evidence isn't one hundred per cent accurate, someone who could take the first five or six pieces of information may decide it's not for him after the seventh piece and not put up a hand. You should be able to place a communication with no more than four or five pieces of really specific information. Let spirit know that you'd like details such as their relationship to the recipient, age on passing, and the work they did, and leave the full description of the personality until after you have placed the contact.

If you're just throwing out the information, and you have two or three people who can take everything and you truly can't feel which one you are with, ask spirit for a piece of evidence that only one of them can take. When one says "yes" to it, check with the others that they can't take it before you continue.

Once you've identified the correct recipient, you will feel the energy start to grow. Before continuing, thank the other person or people who have been working with you, in order to cut the energetic link with them.

Very occasionally, someone will recognise a contact and acknowledge that they know who it is but won't want to take it any further. I remember one occasion when a woman's abusive ex-husband came through and she refused the communication. This is why, after identifying the recipient, some mediums will say "Is it all right to work with you?" before continuing. If the recipient says that she doesn't want a message from the person who's come through, it is vital that you accept this with good grace and understanding. You may be aware that the person has come through to ask the recipient to forgive him, but you should avoid saying this because you don't know what he did in life to hurt the recipient, or the mental scars that remain. Say something along the lines of "That's fine. I quite understand." and leave it at that. Anything else could just be rubbing salt in the wound, or could leave the recipient feeling guilty for rejecting the communication.

9
USING YOUR MEDIUMSHIP:

Evidence – The Message

EVIDENCE

There are three schools of thought concerning how to get evidence. One is to ask questions of spirit – "How old were you when you passed?", "What job did you do?", "How many children did you have?" and so on. I remember doing an exercise, a number of years ago, with one tutor, where our sole remit was to talk about how music had affected the communicator's life. So we asked "What was your favourite type of music?", "Is there a particular memory associated with music?" "Did you play a musical instrument?" and whatever else occurred to us along those lines. One problem with this method is that, as in life, there may be some questions that the communicator doesn't want to answer, or areas of his life that he'd rather not revisit. Not only may this result in our wasting valuable energy trying to look for the answer, but if an answer doesn't come through, our brains may step in and start to give us what we think it 'should' be.

The second method is just to open up to spirit and accept what comes in. This can be scary, as we are less in control than with the question method. In everyday life, if we ask someone a question, we expect an answer whereas experience tells us that just sitting quietly and looking interested doesn't guarantee that the other person will speak to us!

With the third method, before we start – before getting the link, even – we tell spirit the sort of information we'd like to get – names, perhaps, or information about the person's work or home or hobbies. And then we stop asking and just open up to spirit. I have tried all three methods, and they have all worked for me, but the best information seems to come with the third one.

Whichever method we use, once we've received a piece of information, it's important not just to leave it there and go on to the next. Doing that simply results in a list of facts – for example "he passed at 79 from a heart attack, he was a lawyer, he was married with two sons, and he liked watching football". While all these things may be correct, they're unconnected and so are not telling us anything about what made the person tick. And unless we can get across the personality of the communicator, we are not doing our job properly.

Drilling down

Drilling down into the information (not by asking spirit questions but just by saying to them "tell me more about that") will give a lot more evidence. And picturing or feeling what the person was like in the context of a particular event or activity will help to get information about his or her personality.

So, taking the example of "he passed at 79 from a heart attack" – by focusing on that, we may become aware that he didn't like to be ill and when he started to get chest pain he refused to see a doctor, with the result that, having had the attack, he was rushed to hospital in an ambulance and passed the next day. Or we may become aware, when we start to focus on the fact that "he liked watching football" that there was a particular team he supported and that he usually went to watch matches with his brother who lived in the next street. From dry facts, suddenly we're getting a sense of the man and who he was.

A few years ago at AFC, John Johnson gave a wonderful demonstration of how drilling down can completely change the quality of the information. He got one of the students up on the platform and asked her to work until he clapped his hands. She started to describe a woman and the information she gave was taken by someone in the group. Then she commented that this woman "liked to sew". Immediately, John clapped his hands.

He then asked the student to immerse herself in the image of this woman sewing and to see, or become aware of, what sort of thing she sewed. The student said she made her own clothes. That was accepted by the recipient. John asked if the student saw her sewing by hand or using a machine and, if the latter, whether it was electric or manual. Again the answer was accepted as correct. After this, John asked the student to look around and see where the sewing was done – a special sewing room, the kitchen table, the dining table? – and to notice what else was on the table, and where the woman put the machine when it wasn't in use. All the answers got a "yes" from the recipient and everyone in the group started to get a much clearer picture of the communicator. And all this was done, not by the medium asking questions of spirit, but simply by getting every ounce of information she could out of what the communicator was trying to tell her. It was an excellent demonstration of what we are frequently told – that each piece of information we receive is a story in itself.

Sometimes, this sort of drilling down can be done by focusing on the emotion that is coming through. I did a reading last year where the communicator gave me a sense of being shut in. Concentrating on that feeling led me to the circumstances which resulted in him being physically shut in somewhere shortly before his passing and gave me a lot of important information about him.

It requires energy for spirit to send us evidence, which means that as much information as possible will be crammed into what, on the surface, seems to be just one thing. For example, if you are clairvoyant and you get an image of a photograph, once you've described it, you can get more information by 'zooming out' – describing the frame, then where the photo is kept (on a shelf perhaps, or on a piano or a windowsill). If it's on a piano, can you see someone playing the piano, and what sort of music is she playing? Which room is the photo in – sitting room, bedroom, kitchen? What is the room like? Is there anything special that spirit is drawing your attention to? You might even be able to see what is outside the window, so as to get an idea of where this house or apartment is. Look at any clocks in the room to see what time they're showing, or any newspapers for dates – all these may be relevant. From one image – that of the photograph – you can become aware of a huge amount of information.

Similarly, if you were to get an image of a man with a limp, allow yourself to become aware of what caused this, what sort of injury it was, and where and when it happened. From this you might discover that he had a love of skiing or, if the injury happened at work, it could lead you into information about the sort of work he did.

Being specific

We all know about clairvoyance and clairaudience and clairsentience. But there's another 'clair' that AFC tutors frequently mention – and that's 'clairvagueness'. This is something that needs to be avoided at all costs. The more specific we can be, the more impressive and, more to the point, more valuable the message will be.

So, we should never just say "he's showing me a dog" without going on to describe the dog. And even for someone like me who knows very little about different breeds of dog, it's still not too difficult to talk about the size and colour of the animal, the type of tail, the ears and the length of the snout.

Similarly, if you see a watch, don't just describe it with the one word. Is it a gold watch, a silver watch or perhaps even a Mickey Mouse watch? Does it have a strap and, if so, is that made of metal or leather or plastic?

Remember, too, that words can mean different things to different people. Someone who lives in a house with five bedrooms and three reception rooms and someone who lives in a one room apartment may well disagree about what constitutes a 'big' house. Phrases such as 'living in the country' need to be qualified – did she live on a farm, in a village in a rural setting, or in a cottage miles from anywhere? The possibilities are numerous.

Another frequently used phrase is "he worked with his hands". But that can mean almost anything. He may have been a manual labourer but, equally, he may have been a barber or a silversmith or a dog groomer.

If you describe someone as having a love of reading, what sort of thing did she read – fiction, non-fiction? And what type of fiction or non-fiction? It's the same with other hobbies – what sort of music did he enjoy, what sort of embroidery did she do, what sort of sport did she take part in, what sort of things did he like to cook? And, of course, what sort of television programmes did she like – or did she not watch television?

And, since the communicator has already given you the initial piece of evidence, you can be sure that this additional information is there for the taking, if you just open your mind to it.

In the same way that the single words 'dog', 'watch', 'sport' and so on need to be elaborated on, so, too, do common single names. For example, I suspect that almost everyone over the age of about thirty knows a 'John' in spirit, so just the name without any other information isn't good evidence. Nor, of course, is just a single initial - "I'm getting a name beginning with 'J'".

When describing the illness a person passed with, we should try to be as specific as possible – not dwelling on the symptoms, which could well be distressing for the recipient, but naming the type of illness. In other words, not just 'cancer' but breast cancer or prostate cancer or lung cancer. Not just 'chest problems' but a heart condition, or a lung condition. And was the illness long term or did it come on suddenly? However, if you are talking about the passing – particularly if it was difficult or if it came at the end of a long illness, it's vital to tell the recipient that the communicator is now quite free of pain or symptoms of any kind. If the person was in a coma before passing, it is also important that you don't imply that he knew what was happening at that time – although, of course, he knows now.

Occasionally, you may get more information than you want with respect to the person's death (particularly if it was an accident or suicide). This is probably the only situation where it's important not to be too specific. Describing something horrifying in graphic detail is totally unnecessary and lacking in compassion for the recipients. Spirit will have given you the details for your own information, not so that you can talk about it. It's quite enough to say "I know that he died when his car skidded on the ice and crashed into a tree". And Kitty Woud suggests that, in a demonstration, it might be better to say "he died in tragic circumstances" rather than "he committed suicide". You don't have to describe the communicator's terrible injuries in the accident or his state of mind when he killed himself. We don't have to repeat everything that spirit tells us – if it seems that something might distress the recipient, the best thing is not to say it.

Avoiding 'non-information'

Some mediums, especially those who are just starting to train, will give a lot of what I would call 'non-information'. These are the sort of things that, while they may be perfectly accurate, are not helpful to identify the person who has come through. For example, "he's about 5 foot 7 tall". Well I, for one, have no idea how tall my relatives were in feet and inches. I know roughly if they were taller or shorter than me, but that's it. Similarly, "he's of average build". What does that mean? What is average? And was he of 'average build' throughout his life or were there times when he was heavier or lighter?

Another one is "she has brown hair". Is this dark brown, light brown? And at what stage of her life was her hair brown? Did it turn grey later in life and, if so, did the recipient know her only when she had brown hair? This is particularly relevant nowadays when a lot of women dye their hair – and may well change its colour from time to time.

Simone Key says that this sort of information isn't actually being given to us by spirit. What we're doing when we give descriptions, she says, is 'psychometrising' the communicator – in other words, we are reading their energy psychically. And the more you do this, the more energy you are using up, which you could use more productively to acquire really specific evidence from spirit.

A description of clothes is 'non information' unless you're seeing a uniform or you're absolutely certain that the communicator seldom, if ever, wore anything different from what you're being shown (for example, "she always wore pink" or "he always wore tweed suits with a waistcoat").

Some years ago, in a group at AFC, John Johnson went round the class asking each of us to describe ourselves in one or two sentences, as we would if we were in spirit and trying to identify ourselves to a loved one through a medium. No one mentioned their build or their hair, other than one woman who had unusually long red hair. Everyone mentioned the less usual things in their lives – a female doctor who wore green nail varnish, a writer of children's books who collected teapots, a mother of five who ran marathons.

Some tutors suggest that we should only give physical descriptions if there is something unusual in the person's appearance – for example, if he or she was very tall or very small, or extremely thin or considerably overweight. If a woman had blue streaks in her hair for much of her adult life or if a man had a Mohican haircut when at university, these observations can be valuable evidence. Similarly, most people over the age of 40 wear glasses but if someone wore glasses with bright red and blue striped frames, this is good evidence.

It can be helpful to think about how you would describe yourself in two sentences if you wanted to be recognised by someone.

Also, under the 'non-information' heading, I should mention guides. Talking about someone's guides is not evidence and should be avoided in an evidential reading. Apart from the fact that some people may not be interested in their guides, there is no way that information about them can be confirmed.

Interpretation

The basic rule concerning interpreting the information we receive is – don't! It doesn't matter if it makes no sense to us as long as it means something to the recipient. And, if you hear something or if spirit puts words into your head, repeat them exactly as they were given to you because there may be a reason for this. For example, if you get "I loved walking in the rain" and you give it as "he loved to walk in the rain", you may get a "no" from the recipient because what the communicator was actually telling you was that "Walking in the rain" was his favourite song.

Eileen Davies tells a lovely story of describing a gentleman in spirit during a demonstration and the phrase came to her that he was "a bit of a James Bond". Now, immediately, she had a picture of someone very suave, a bit of a ladies' man, very charming and so on. But she knew that that was her own interpretation, so she just said to the recipient "he tells me he was a bit of a James Bond". The recipient smiled and said "yes" and Eileen went on to what the communicator was telling her next. After the demonstration, the recipient (who was the wife of the gentleman in question) came up to Eileen and said "I laughed at you describing him like that, but you were absolutely right – he was a spy." It turned out that her husband had worked for British intelligence and so it was that aspect of James Bond that he was commenting on.

Using symbols

The language of spirit, says John Johnson, is shorthand. Communicating requires a lot of energy which means that as much information as possible is crammed into everything we receive. It's then up to us to feel what exactly is being conveyed to us through an image or a sound or a feeling. This is why some mediums like to set up a system of symbols that they pre-arrange with spirit – for example, a cake for a birthday (with the candles lit if the birthday is coming up and unlit if it's in the past), an apple to signify a teacher, confetti to indicate a wedding and so on.

The only problem with this is that you have to remember what it is that you've arranged. So, while it may seem like a good way of working, it's probably only helpful for those mediums with excellent memories.

However, we can also work with symbols in a more limited way. This is mainly useful for relationships and occupations. We can arrange with spirit that, if someone is, say, uncle on mother's side of the family, we will see an uncle who was on our mother's side of the family. Of course, we can only do this with relatives we actually have. If your mother is an only child, it won't work in this particular instance!

Similarly, if you have a grandfather who was a carpenter, you can arrange with spirit that you will see him if the communicator was a carpenter. If you have a wide range of friends and relatives in different trades and professions, this can be useful.

Relationships

We are frequently told how important it can be to get the relationship right as it may be the piece of evidence that allows the recipient to identify the communicator. (There's a tendency for people to think only of their immediate family members or those whom they want to come through, so they may fail to identify someone who was a neighbour, a colleague or a teacher until you give them the relationship.)

However, despite the importance, a lot of mediums struggle to get relationships. It is particularly hard to get those relationships that you, personally, have never had. So if, like me, you have no brothers or sisters, you may find it difficult to pick up the 'feeling' of a brother or sister and you need to ask spirit to give you the information in a different way. But even with the sort of relationships we've known, it may be hard to identify correctly. For example, if someone feels 'like a mother', she wasn't necessarily the recipient's mother. She may have been her grandmother or stepmother or mother-in-law or godmother, or someone whom the recipient viewed as a mother or 'second mother'.

In-laws are also hard to define but, mostly, this doesn't matter too much because a brother-in-law described as a brother, or a sister-in-law described as a sister is likely to be recognised and accepted.

A valuable lesson was learned by everyone in the group I was in on a recent course at AFC. The student on the platform had brought through a grandfather but became confused because she felt that he passed in his early twenties. She began to doubt that this was, in fact, grandfather and started to second guess herself. However, it turned out that the recipient's grandfather had been a (very young) soldier who was killed shortly after his son (the recipient's father) was born. It's important that we don't assume that grandparents were middle aged or elderly when they passed – they could have been in their twenties, or even their late teens.

Categories of evidence

There's a vast range of good evidence available to us if we're prepared to open up to it:

- **Personality.** While it's possible that there are two people in the audience who have, for example, an aunt in spirit who was a maths teacher and mother of three, it is unlikely that both aunts would have the same personality. Getting a feeling of the personality of the communicator is vital to 'bringing that person to life' and locating the correct recipient. But, while an indication of the personality should come at the start ("she was quite timid", "she was larger than life"), the full description of the personality is better left until after the message has been placed. Sometimes people who come through had unpleasant personalities. In such a case, it's important to describe them as they are now, as well, so that recipients aren't nervous about meeting them again when they, in turn, pass to spirit.

- **Relationship.** Again, this is important in placing the message. A description may sound exactly like my mother but if the medium says this is a woman who has come through to speak to her old school friend, then I know the message isn't for me. To be even more specific, qualify the relationship – if a father or mother comes through, does he or she want to speak to a son or a daughter? If it's an aunt, grandparent, cousin or other relative, which side of the family was he or she on?

- **Family.** Was the communicator married? How many children did she have? Was this a close knit family, living near other relatives? What did the family members do together? How did they get on together?

- **Location.** Where did the person live? Was it a house, an apartment, a bedsit, a caravan, a boat? Be open to the unusual! And did he live in the country or a town, or perhaps move from one to the other at some point? What was the home like – tidy or untidy, painted in bright colours or rather sober, with modern furniture or antiques?

- **Education.** What education did the communicator have? Was it just the basics or did she go to university or do some sort of specific professional training?

- **Work.** What work did the person do? If you get an impression of office work or manual work, drill down – what did the work involve?

- **Food.** What sort of food did he like or dislike?

- **Travel.** Did the person travel? And, if so, where and why (holiday, work, emigration)?

- **Religion.** Did the person have any religious beliefs? If so, what were they? Would she, when incarnate, have been sympathetic towards Spiritualism?

- **Reading.** Did he read much? If so, what? Newspapers, books? Which sections of the newspapers (news, sport, cartoons, crossword)? And what type of books? If fiction, what type? If non-fiction, what subjects?

- **Activities.** What did she love doing? Was there anything she was passionate about?

- **Interests.** What interests did the person share with the recipient? What did they talk about or do together?

- **Pets.** Did the communicator keep dogs (if so, what breeds?) or cats (Persian, Siamese or tabby moggies?). Or did he like more unusual pets such as reptiles or tropical fish?

- **Heirlooms.** What does the recipient have that belonged to the person? Like everything else, this needs to be specific – not just "a ring" but "a silver ring with a blue stone", not just "a box" but "a box made of dark wood, with a carved top and a brass handle".

- **Significant names and dates.** The names may be of people or pets or even places that were important to the communicator. Dates may relate to birthdays, anniversaries of passing, weddings or other significant events.

- **Age when the communicator died.** While this can be a valuable piece of information, it may be better to be slightly more non-specific on this than with other evidence. The reason is that, if you're not absolutely accurate, the information may be rejected – for example, "No, he didn't die when he was 61. He was 62." – whereas if you had said "He passed in his early sixties" it would have been accepted. Remember, too, that if you get an age and it's not the age when the person died, it may be significant for another reason - perhaps that was when he got sick, or when his wife died or something else that, in his mind, he associated with his eventual demise.

- **How the communicator passed** – illness, accident, suicide, murder? If an accident, what sort (but avoid giving gory details). If an illness, how long? Some people in spirit don't want to talk about how they passed, so this information isn't always available. However, if you're a nurse or a doctor, this may be the first thing that they tell you. If you do have medical training, try to be specific about the illness – be aware of the symptoms and make a diagnosis! Identifying correctly that the person had Parkinson's disease or vascular dementia or septicaemia is great evidence.

- **Sayings and catchphrases.** It's not just people on television who have catchphrases. When I was a child, our very busy neighbour was always running late. "I'm all behind, like a cow's tail" was a favourite saying of hers. Terms of endearment can also be good evidence – a friend of mine used to call all her friends "ducky", another called everyone "darling", while a third called her daughter "kitten".

- **Things happening in the recipient's life** that the communicator is aware of. "You've been redecorating your bedroom and your Mum says plain curtains would have looked better than patterned" is a great piece of evidence when the recipient knows that that is exactly what her mother would say.

THE MESSAGE

Some mediums, who have no problems at all when it comes to getting evidence, find getting a message difficult. The most helpful piece of advice I've been given on this is "the message is in the evidence". Allow your mind to run briefly over the evidence you have given, and the message should come easily.

Very often it is to do with the communicator's personality. If she was someone who was very supportive of the recipient in life, then that support will still be there. But it is important, if she has come to offer support, that you say something about why the recipient needs it at this time. Spirit will give you this information so, for example, the message might be "She knows that your mum is ill at the moment and that you're doing a great job in looking after her. But she wants to remind you that you don't have to do it all yourself and that you need to make sure you look after yourself as well."

On one occasion I brought through an uncle who was a great family man and was very close to both the recipient and her brother. He wanted to tell his niece that he knew the two of them had fallen out – and to suggest that it was about time they made up! Coming from her uncle, whom she loved dearly, the recipient was able to accept this and told me later that she had rung her brother that night, and all was now well.

Remember, too, that the evidence includes all the feelings and emotions that you've been aware of. A feeling of deep love for and connection with the recipient may mean that the person just wants to say "I'm here and I love you." Indeed, the message itself may come as an emotion, such as regret. In such a case, the communicator may be seeking the recipient's forgiveness. However, you should never pass this on because the recipient may not be ready to forgive, and a request for forgiveness may cause anger or distress. It is, though, perfectly acceptable to say something along the lines of "He wants you to know that he now regrets what he did".

If the communicator has passed recently, the message may just be an assurance to the recipient that he or she has 'arrived safely' and is free from pain or other symptoms of the final illness.

The message should always be uplifting and reassuring, and it should help the recipient to move on. It should be concise and should never be longer than the evidence. It can, however, be evidential in itself if it's to do with what's going on in the recipient's life at the moment. And this aspect is very important, because the message is all about the Fourth Principle of Spiritualism (the continuous existence of the human soul) – demonstrating that the person who has passed over is still involved in the recipient's life.

Rebecca Sawyer, a wonderful medium who I've had the privilege of meeting several times at AFC, tells the story of something that happened when she was giving a public demonstration:

> A young man of 25 came through for his family of Mum, Dad, sister and other relatives all sitting in the front row. He had passed suddenly and without warning four months ago. When he said "Mum you have got to stop polishing that photo every day, it's going to wear away", it highlighted the magic of spirit. She looked at me and said "I really, really hate housework but, I must polish that photo and hold it at least twice a day". Within that simple message and reunion with his Mum he was sharing, "Mum.....LOOK.....mum..... I am here"

Sometimes in the message, spirit will give advice or encouragement to do something (such as the uncle who wanted to effect a reconciliation between his niece and her brother). But beware of saying "you must" or "you should". Spirit will only ever make a suggestion. Making it sound like an instruction is the medium's doing. And it has been known for mediums to be sued by clients for telling them that they must do something, if the results have been less than successful.

Accuracy while giving the message is just as important as it is while giving evidence. As one tutor said "Don't give a message that you think the recipient wants to hear. Listen to what spirit is saying and relay that to the recipient."

Be in the power and let it flow

When all's said and done, if we can get fully into the power and trust to spirit, that is when the best information and messages will come through – and we may not even realise it. Chris Drew tells a wonderful story about doing a public demonstration on one occasion and a woman, whose brother had been brought through, coming up to him afterwards. "Do you know sign language?" she asked. Chris said that he didn't. "Well," said the woman, "My brother's daughter is deaf and, just as you finished talking about him, your hands spelled out "I love you" in sign language."

10
USING YOUR MEDIUMSHIP:

Language – Dealing with "No" – Techniques

NOT JUST WHAT WE SAY,
BUT HOW WE SAY IT

Even if our evidence is accurate and of high quality, we can spoil a demonstration or reading by using language that makes it seem less so. I don't mean bad language – although if a communicator comes through in a demonstration and intersperses what he's saying with swear words, his communication should not be given verbatim! Nor, of course, should his use of language be ignored, but it's enough to say something along the lines of "He liked using the odd expletive" or "His language tended to be colourful".

But what this section is about is precision of language so that it clarifies, rather than obscures, what we are trying to get across.

So, for example, right at the start, if you're going direct to someone in the audience, it's best to avoid the phrase "I'm drawn to the lady (or gentleman) at the back (or wherever)" because it suggests that you're working psychically. And anyway, as I've already said, most AFC tutors like you to get some evidence first, before you place your contact.

Once you have thrown your information out, and perhaps identified the area of the room that your recipient is in, it's better to ask "Where am I?" rather than "Who understands this?" The latter allows for the possibility that nobody can, whereas the former lets the audience know that you are certain that someone will be able to take the evidence.

Demonstrations and readings should be all about spirit, not about the medium who is giving them. And so we need to use language that focuses on spirit and not on us. Rather than saying "I'm seeing . . ." or "I'm smelling . . ." (which, apart from anything else, takes time and brings in the analytical part of our brains), just give the evidence – "She always had flowers around the house" or "She wore a perfume that smelled like roses".

Never use "I'm hearing . . ." unless you truly are clairaudient. If you say you have heard something and it's not accurate, the recipient will start to doubt you, because why would the communicator say something that's incorrect? The same applies to "She's saying . . ." since this, too, implies that you have actually heard the words. It's better to say "She's telling me . . ." because it's perfectly possible to be told something through a picture or a feeling. And the best phrase of all is "She wants to tell you . . ." because it then becomes about the communicator and the recipient rather than about the communicator and you. If you're not absolutely sure about the piece of evidence, using the phrase "She's giving me the impression that . . ." offers you a little wiggle room if what you're saying turns out to be not quite right. And, of course, never say "I think . . ." Not only does it suggest uncertainty but it can switch your mind from receptive mode into logical, thinking mode.

Once you've established who the communicator is, use their relationship to the recipient rather than "this man" or "this woman". "Your dad liked to play golf" is much better than "This man liked to play golf". If you were talking to someone about her father who was still here on earth, you'd never refer to him as "this man" – so why do it when the person is in spirit?

It's also important to keep reminding your audience who it is that's giving you the information. "Your mum is showing me . . .", "Your mum used to do such-and-such . . .", "Your mum liked . . ." Constant use of "I feel", "I'm aware" and so on, without reference to the person who is giving you the information can take the power from spirit and make it harder for them to communicate.

Try to use a variety of different ways to express the same thing – "he's showing me . . .", "your dad's telling you . . .", "he's making me aware of" and so on – in order to stop your delivery from becoming monotonous.

One of the first things we learn at AFC (if we don't already know it) is not to ask the recipient questions. If we want people to believe that we are getting our information from spirit (which, hopefully, we are!) we don't want to give the impression that we're fishing for answers from the recipients.

Even the question "Would you understand . . .?" is best avoided because it can lower the energy by suggesting uncertainty, while turning the phrase around and saying "You would understand . . ." will raise the energy. However, if you've given a piece of evidence and want to make sure that the recipient has understood it, it's better to ask "Do you understand that?" rather than "Does that make sense?" since the latter implies that you could have expressed it better.

And, above all, it's essential to sound confident (even if you're not). If you use the words "possibly" or "probably" or "it may be", not only are you telling yourself that you're not right, you're telling the audience that you're not confident in your own abilities. And you need to be careful that your tone of voice and your facial expression don't give the game away when you're feeling unsure. Look confident and sound confident – even if you're not.

Never tell the audience what you don't know – for example "I don't know how many children she had" or "I'm not sure if she had a job". The audience needs to believe that you know everything, even if you're not saying it.

If you get something but don't know how it fits or if it's significant, don't say "You wouldn't understand such-and-such, would you?" Just give the information as you get it. It's the recipient who decides whether something's significant, not you. However, negative evidence can be as valuable as positive so, if you know where something *doesn't* fit, it's perfectly all right to say something along the lines of "He's showing me a horse but I know that he didn't ride."

Try to avoid saying "er" or "um" or repeatedly using a word or phrase such as "OK", "All right", or "I mean . . ." Not only are these irritating to listen to but, if you say them too often, your audience will end up listening to those words (and counting how many times you say them!) rather than listening to the evidence you're giving.

Speak in everyday language. Avoid describing communicators as male or female energies. They're men and women. Avoid referring to "a father figure" – he's a father, or perhaps a grandfather. And don't speak about the "earth plane". It's the earth. Not only is this sort of esoteric language outdated but it is likely to confuse people who have never before seen a medium work and they may not come back.

And finally, listen to the words you're using because they may have deeper significance than you realise when you're saying them. Some years ago, demonstrating in the library at AFC, I brought through a gentleman who, I said, loved books. I then said "He would have loved this library". If I'd gone into it slightly deeper, I would have realised that he had been a tutor at AFC and he had loved this library. Similarly, I was doing a private reading on one occasion and brought through a lady who wanted to show me where she lived. I described a very peaceful atmosphere and lots of polished wood – and then I said "But if feels rather enclosed." It was only when the recipient laughed and said "exactly right" that I realised that what the communicator was trying to tell me was that she was a nun in an enclosed order.

DEALING WITH 'NO'

None of us likes to get things wrong . . . and particularly not if we're standing on a platform in front of an audience. But it happens, and even the very best mediums can't get things right all the time. So, when someone says "No" to us, we need to be able to deal with it.

There are some mediums who, having got a "no", just plough on regardless, with a different piece of information. Personally, I feel this is discourteous – to spirit who was trying to tell them something that they misinterpreted, and to the recipient who is left feeling that the medium wasn't listening to her.

One way to deal with a "no" is to say "But you do understand . . ." and then repeat the last piece of information to which there was a "yes". This allows the recipient to know that we were listening, but still means there's a piece of information that spirit tried to tell us and we didn't get.

Some people suggest that, if it was important, spirit will offer the information to us a different way so we should just acknowledge that we got it wrong, hand it back to spirit and go on to something else.

However, some years back, in John Johnson's group at AFC, I learned the technique that I have used ever since. John said "Spirit has no reason to lie. So the information must be correct. What is wrong is the way we've expressed it. What we need to do is change the wording, not the information." So, for example, if I believe that what I'm getting is that the communicator lived by the sea and the recipient says "No", I'll go back and look at how I got the information. Perhaps I felt a love of the sea and saw a house beside the sea. So I'll say "But you'd understand that he loved the sea?" And when the recipient says "yes" to that it may well trigger the true meaning of what I'm being shown which is that the communicator dreamed of living by the sea but never had the opportunity.

One specific situation where we may get a "no", although we're quite sure our evidence is right, is to do with the marital status of the communicator. If you feel that he or she was single but the recipient says "no", it's doesn't necessarily mean that you were wrong. Investigate why you feel that the person was single – was there ill feeling between the man and his wife, so much so that they rarely talked to each other? Or maybe they were divorced, or the partner died at an early age and the communicator lived alone for many years. It pays to drill down rather than just accepting that you got it wrong.

Another situation where we may get a "no" despite the fact that the information is absolutely correct is when we have failed to recognise that the communicator is telling us something not about himself but about the recipient.

Being able to deal confidently with a "no" means that you'll never again be scared of getting it wrong. Our tutors aren't scared of making mistakes because they know it's inevitable on occasion. As Sharon Harvey has said "If you get something wrong . . . so what?" But what the tutors also know is that, after a demonstration or a reading, while the medium will remember what he or she got wrong, the recipient will remember everything that was right.

TIPS AND TECHNIQUES

Enjoy your mediumship! If you do, your audience will feel your enjoyment and be able to share your pleasure at bringing through their friends and relatives. Right at the start of your demonstration or reading tell yourself "I am competent and I am capable". Remember to keep your head up as this helps to keep your energy and your confidence up, and don't shut your eyes. Shutting our eyes is quite a natural reaction when we're asked to think hard about something. But, of course, mediumship is not about thinking, and shutting our eyes will take us into ourselves rather than out towards spirit. Instead, try to keep your eyes focused on something – the back of the room in a demonstration or a point just over the sitter's head in a private reading. Eventually it becomes possible, in a demonstration, to do what experienced public speakers do – to look out at the audience without focusing on any particular person, but making it appear to each one of them that you are connecting with them personally. One tutor has advised that we should be at one spiritually with the communicator and mentally with the recipient while distancing ourselves spiritually from the recipient and mentally from the communicator.

Try to find the connections between the things that spirit is telling you, so that you can tell a story. But don't get into a long story right at the beginning because, if any of it is incorrect, the recipient may think it's for someone else.

Two communicators

One thing that can be confusing is when two communicators come in together. As Sharon Harvey commented "Spirit can be like Tesco and offer you two for one!" When this occurs, it's often two people who were closely associated when they were on earth. As soon as you're aware that this has happened, ask one to step back and work with each in turn. Sometimes it can take some time before you're aware of it though, especially if they are the same gender. On many occasions I've only realised it when the recipient has said "I think you've got my father and my grandfather there" (or "my mother and my mother-in-law" or whatever it happens to be). Sometimes you'll be alerted to the situation because, after saying "yes" a number of times, the recipient suddenly starts saying "no". Be aware that, in any situation, if you get a "no" more than twice in a row, another communicator may have come in or you may be with the wrong recipient.

Sometimes people who were close when on earth can come through together for different people if both have relatives or friends in the audience. For example, one tutor experienced a teenage boy and girl coming through at the same time because they had died together in a road accident, and both their mothers were at the demonstration.

Because it takes energy for spirit to communicate with us, two people who are unconnected to each other but who have very similar life stories and personalities may come through together for two different recipients. A clue that this has happened is when you get piece after piece of good evidence and two people in the audience keep saying "yes". Sometimes they look over at each other and say "Are we related?" because the similarities can be quite extraordinary.

I know some people have doubts as to whether this does really happen – whether there are, in fact, two communicators there. But some time ago, in a seminar run by Eileen Davies, we did an experiment. There were twelve of us in the class and each one in turn got up and put out the intent to spirit that we wanted to link to two people who were very similar, who had friends or relatives among the class members. And every single one of us managed it. I still remember my demonstration. I got a girl who had passed suddenly from an illness at the age of 12. Up till then she had been perfectly healthy and was very bright academically. She was taken into hospital and died three days later, while her parents sat with her. And two people – out of an audience of only eleven – could take everything I said. So I have no doubt that this happens!

Getting emotional

Sometimes, when the communicator's story is powerful, the medium can feel quite emotional. However, we can't start crying on the platform . . . or even in a private reading. The way to deal with this is to acknowledge the emotion, use its energy, tell the recipient what you're feeling ("I'm aware of a great deal of sadness here . . .", or "He's allowing me to share the pride and joy he felt on this occasion . . .") and then ask spirit to remove the feeling from you. Do exactly the same if you get physical symptoms from spirit – describe what you're experiencing – "I'm feeling that he had severe chest pain" (or abdominal pain or shortness of breath or whatever the symptoms are) and then ask spirit to take the sensation away. Never allow the emotion or the pain to swamp you, as not only is it very unpleasant but you are likely to lose the contact.

If a recipient is starting to get emotional, check whether she wants you to continue and, if she does, ask spirit for a memory that will make her laugh, in order to lift the energy.

Similarly, if a particular contact in a demonstration has been all about doom and gloom (apart from the message, of course), ask for the next communicator to be more light-hearted so the energy will be raised.

When the recipient doesn't know

Occasionally someone will come in who the recipient didn't know well – a grandfather or a great-aunt, perhaps. In such a case, ask spirit to bring in someone connected with the communicator who the recipient would know better.As well as people who the recipient didn't know well, you may get information that he or she doesn't know and that will need to be researched. This can be amazingly evidential (and when the recipient gets in touch to tell you that you were absolutely right, it can be a huge boost to your self confidence) but it's important to ask spirit not to include too much information that needs research or your audience will start to think that you're just making stuff up.

Using fillers

Most of the tutors at AFC use 'fillers'. These are phrases such as "He's showing me . . ." or "He's making me aware of . . .", that you say even before you've been shown something or been made aware of something, because it lets spirit know that you're waiting for information – and, as you say it, something will come into your mind. You can do this right at the start of your demonstration – say "I have here . . ." without pausing to think – and you'll know whether you have a man, a woman or a child.

And if, as sometimes happens, you've been shown something and you've described it but you aren't sure of its significance, another useful filler is "The reason he's showing me this is . . ."

Ages, dates and places

Simone Key teaches that if you can get "an anniversary in January", you can get the exact date of the anniversary, and that if you can get "he passed in his seventies", you can get his exact age.

I have been taught two ways of finding dates. One is to visualise a long thin calendar, to note the month, and to see which day jumps out at you. The other is to get the month first, then get a sense of whether you want the beginning, middle or end of the month, and finally to get the exact date.

To ask someone if a certain month has significance for him is not evidence. I can think of significant things affecting my immediate family that occurred in eight different months. If someone has a large family, there are likely to be significant anniversaries (birthdays, marriages and deaths) in every month.

Once you have found the date (or at least the month and whether it's beginning, middle or end) it's important to say what sort of anniversary it is – a sad one or a happy one.

When it comes to places, Simone Key maintains that if you 'look' at a map in your mind, it can take you to within five miles of where the person lived. Of course, this is probably easier when you're demonstrating in a church where you can be pretty sure that everyone listening to you is fairly local, rather than at AFC where you'd have to picture a map of the world! Nonetheless, if you are working with a multinational audience, it should still be possible to get a sense of which continent the communicator came from, which will cut down the number of possible recipients.

More advice from the tutors

If you get what seems to be a strong and specific piece of evidence but the recipient can't take it in relation to the communicator, see where else it might fit into the recipient's life. For example, you may get an image of a yellow child's bicycle with a teddy bear in the basket. If this wasn't the communicator's, was it the recipient's? Or did it belong to another member of the family who the communicator wants to talk about? If it was a really clear image, you can be fairly sure that it will fit somewhere!

If you're fortunate enough to be clairaudient, don't just listen to the words of the communicator. Listen to his or her accent. Listen to whether he uses a dialect or slang of some sort. All of these will help you to place where he came from and are valuable evidence.

The 'clairs' that are strongest will vary over time and from contact to contact. We need to be open to all the ways in which spirit can communicate with us and to be aware of how they are offering us information.

There is no area of evidence that you can't get. A lot of people, for example, say "I never get names" or "I can't get names" and this becomes a self-fulfilling prophecy because spirit hears and thinks "Well, in that case, we won't give you any names." If you're open to all types of information, you will get all types of information. Admittedly, certain communicators may not want to tell you about some aspect of their lives, but that doesn't mean that other communicators will be reticent about that aspect.

Conversely, be careful what you ask spirit for. Years ago, Simone Key asked to get more names – and suddenly she found she was awash with names, getting about thirty for every demonstration. If you really want to get more names, try using people's names more often in everyday life, and familiarise yourself with names by looking through some 'what to call your baby' books.

If a communication is flagging, try looking at the relationship that the recipient had with the communicator, or take your awareness to what you're feeling and see what that feeling is telling you.

People often talk about bringing spirit close but, if you've made your link, you are already close. All you have to do is to step into their energy. If they're still feeling distant, it's to do with their personality. It may help to concentrate on your solar plexus which, according to Gordon Higginson, is the seat of our power, in order to get closer to them, or you may want to bring in someone more communicative instead.

No matter how many mistakes we make, spirit will always be there for us. If we believe spirit will give us an answer, it will. Because we don't work *for* the spirit world, we work *with* it. It's a partnership of minds, we are all equal and we are the team's 'local rep'.

Mediumship isn't about being comfortable – we need to stretch ourselves. As Sandie Baker has said "Come out of the comfort zone and move into the magic".

And finally, remember that the point of mediumship is not just to demonstrate survival but to show how spirit can help people to cope with life in the here and now.

11

USING YOUR MEDIUMSHIP:

Presentation – Demonstrating in Public

PRESENTATION

It's not just staying in the power and getting a link that's important. Good presentation is essential on the platform. Your first message has got to grab the attention of the audience and, if you're hesitant or unsure of yourself, you could lose both the audience and the energy and it will be very hard to reclaim them. This is why tutors always tell students not to go on the platform too soon. There are some who after, perhaps, six months of sitting in a circle and having taken one course at AFC consider they are ready to demonstrate publicly. Sadly, all too often they finish up disappointing both their audiences and themselves. The truly great mediums spend years developing. The Scottish medium Gordon Smith spent 15 years in training, while Gordon Higginson, who has been described as a 'spiritual giant' sat in a circle for seven years, learning how to build the power, before even being allowed to give a communication.

Of course, presentation isn't just about evidence. Imagine how you would feel if a medium brought through someone dear to you but delivered the information in a monotonous voice, or so quietly that you could hardly hear? Or if the medium constantly paced up and down the platform, or didn't bother to wait for you to respond? Or if the evidence, even if correct, was just a series of unrelated facts?

There is so much to think about when we are giving a demonstration and perhaps the most important thing is to be aware that we are telling someone's story. As Lynn Probert has said, "It should be like *This is your Life*". In your manner and your presentation you need to show that you care about the people you are communicating with and that you are interested in them.

It's also essential that we get ourselves out of the way when we're demonstrating. A demonstration is not about us, it's about spirit. We are just the channel through which spirit can communicate with a loved one. So we need to allow spirit to lead us and to avoid using "I" too much (such as "I'm seeing", "I'm hearing", "I'm sensing"). We're so used to talking about ourselves in everyday life that this is not easy, but it will come with practice if we remain aware of what we are saying. In addition, never explain to your audience how you got the information ("I saw an image of my cousin Tony, so I knew this was your cousin") as this wastes time and, again, makes it more about you than about spirit.

The focal point of your demonstration must be your mediumship and the story you're telling with the evidence. You, as the medium, should avoid doing anything that might distract the audience from that, such as constantly moving around or using excessive and repetitive hand gestures or repeating words such as "OK" or "I mean". Some mediums tend to become 'larger than life' on the platform, making the whole thing into a performance, with themselves as the stars – but the result of this is that it's the performance, rather than the messages, that people remember. True mediumship isn't about performing – it's about being. If we can just be ourselves on the platform, our light will shine through.

If we get ourselves out of the way, we can become one with spirit and the information will flow. But it's probably best to avoid speaking about spirit in the first person (for example "I went to church every Sunday" or "I loved to grow vegetables in my garden") as not only does this move the focus from spirit to you, but also it can be confusing for anyone who has not heard a medium work before.

Using body language and public speaking skills, try to include the whole audience in what is happening. If you're nervous of public speaking, there is an excellent organisation called Toastmasters International which runs clubs all over the world, helping people to develop communication and public speaking skills. This, of course, isn't just about overcoming nerves but ensuring that you can project your voice to the back of the audience and that you can speak clearly so every word can be heard.

Working with the recipient

Remember that we are not just bringing information through – we are celebrating lives and reuniting loved ones. And such reunions can be emotional. If a recipient starts to cry, ask if she'd like you to stop. She'll probably say "no" but, if you don't ask, other people in the audience will start to think "I don't want the medium coming to me" and this will result in a drop of energy in the room.

It's important, though, to be aware of the sort of thing that might distress recipients or embarrass them and to know what is appropriate to say in a demonstration. If you get something very personal that the recipient would, more than likely, not want other people to know, never say it from the platform, but ask him to have a word with you afterwards. A very good list of 'eight commandments' regarding both platform work and private readings is:

- don't interpret
- don't swear
- don't bully
- don't embarrass
- don't prescribe
- don't predict
- don't philosophise
- don't advise

Of course, it's not just you, the medium, effecting the reunion between spirit and their loved ones. The recipients have a role to play, too. If they don't speak up clearly, ask them "Can you take that?" or "Are you saying yes to that?" and then ask them, if they can, please to speak a little louder so everyone can hear. Always include the "if they can" bit because once in a blue moon you'll get someone who has some sort of impediment which means he can't and then it could be embarrassing. But it's important to get the responses as loud as possible because, otherwise – no matter how good you are – the rest of the audience will get bored because they won't know if you're right or wrong. In addition, a stream of "yeses", clearly spoken, will boost your confidence and raise the energy. However, if the recipient sounds hesitant when saying "yes", ask what she's unsure of and, if you've misunderstood what spirit has told you, go back and get it right.

Some recipients, of course, are only too happy to speak to you and it can be really annoying when they tell you something that you were about to tell them! If they tell you too much before you have a chance to ask them "not to feed the medium" just say

"Now you've told me that, I'll go on to something else". However, Tony Stockwell likes these "mini reveals" as he calls them, saying that, if it reinforces what you have just said, it adds to the impact of the information.

Another slightly tricky situation is if you get a contact for someone you know well or someone with whom you've worked before. In such cases, let the audience know the position and ask the recipient to tell you if you're repeating information you've given him on another occasion. You should also do this with private readings, if a client has seen you before, to enable you to get fresh information and make every reading as good as the first.

A few final pointers

Even though you are working with an individual recipient, you need to remain aware of the rest of the audience. For this reason, you should never step down from the platform as this will result in an immediate drop of energy in the room because some of the audience will be unable to see you, and your proximity to the recipient will make others feel excluded. You also need to be aware of how the audience is feeling. If they're getting bored this may be because you're speaking too slowly or you're repeating yourself. Some repetition is acceptable – such as in a succinct summary of the initial information once it's been taken – but simply repeating a piece of information over and over (as I have heard done although not, of course, at AFC) will just leave the audience wondering "How many ways are there to say he enjoyed a game of cards?"

One absolutely vital rule is never to try to force a contact on someone. If the recipient tells you that he or she doesn't want to hear from the communicator, or doesn't know the communicator, accept this with good grace. I remember, years ago at AFC, we were doing demonstrations in the group. One woman got up and said to the tutor "I have a man here and I know he's for you." She went on to describe the man in detail – and the tutor said he didn't recognise him. She said the man was a cockney and had lived in London all his life – and the tutor said he himself had never lived in London and knew hardly anyone there. And yet the student went on, determined to make it fit. Those of us watching felt embarrassed and were left wondering why she was so determined to give a contact to someone who couldn't take it and whether, in fact she was making the whole thing up.

Finally, when you've given your last message and you're ready to sit down, don't forget to disconnect from spirit. Like making a link, it doesn't need a whole palaver. It's just like putting up the 'closed' sign on a shop door – a mental message to spirit that you are no longer open and that anyone who wants to make contact will have to wait until next time.

DEMONSTRATING IN PUBLIC

When you're demonstrating, always allow plenty of time to get to the venue. You don't want to arrive harassed and out of breath because your train was late or because you've been held up in a traffic jam. And, if you're going by car, check with the organiser whether you need to allow extra time to find somewhere to park.

If you're demonstrating in a hall or in a church that you've not visited before, you'll need to be there early to get the feel of the place and its energies. Check who else is due to be on the platform. Very occasionally (for example, if you've been invited to demonstrate at a charity event) you may find yourself sharing a platform with someone you've come across before and whose way of working is not yours. There are 'mediums' around who work purely on the psychic level or who are simply fortune tellers. If you are not comfortable about seeming to be associated with another medium, ask the organiser if you can remain sitting in the audience until it's your turn to demonstrate.

Even experienced mediums get nervous. But nerves are a form of energy and can be used to support your mediumship rather than detract from it. Remember that, physiologically, exactly the same thing is happening in your body when you're nervous as when you're excited. The only difference is your state of mind. If you really find nerves a problem, try taking four drops of Dr. Bach Rescue Remedy five minutes before you start. If you've not come across it before, this is a flower remedy – perfectly safe but very powerful – which is wonderful for calming nerves.

However, you don't want to be too relaxed so avoid any kind of meditation before you're due to demonstrate. At AFC services, before the mediums get up to work, some lively music is often played, in order to lift the energies in the Sanctuary. This can be especially useful if you are taking a full service in a church and, before your demonstration, have had to give the opening prayer and the address, both of which require calmer energies.

Simone Key has her own method of relieving the anxieties of fledgling mediums before a demonstration. She tells them to get angry! Angry with the church for inviting them to demonstrate, angry with the audience who will be coming to listen and angry with spirit for requiring them to do this! (Fortunately, she says, spirit is very forgiving.) And every time she has suggested this, the demonstration has been first class.

Preparation

If circumstances permit, start to build your power a few hours before your demonstration is due to start. If you're fortunate enough to live near a river, a lake or the sea, have a short walk there, as this will help you to empower. Speak to your guides and ask them to help you in your demonstration. Let them know that you intend to do the very best you can.

However, it's important not to get fully into your power until just before you actually start the demonstration. Going into it too soon will cause you to expend energy that you'll need later on.

Just before you stand up

Ask spirit to help you move fully into your power. Send out love to the entire audience, knowing that there will be people there who are really in need of a communication from a loved one. Send love to the world of spirit, knowing that there are people there who really want to communicate.

Remember that you have given accurate information before (if you haven't, what are you doing on a platform?) and remind yourself that there is no reason why this time should be different. Remember, too, what your job is – it's simply to communicate with spirit and pass on what they want to say to their loved ones. It isn't (although some people may tell you that it is) to prove the existence of the spirit world. If people are adamant non-believers, you could produce the most amazing communication anyone has ever heard and they still wouldn't be convinced. The most that can happen is that, for those who are uncertain but who have open minds, the messages you bring through will help them to start to believe.

You will need to get the attention of the audience with your first contact and, for this reason, it's helpful if your first recipient is sitting towards the back of the hall. So ask spirit to bring through someone who wants to speak to a friend or relative sitting near the back. At the same time, ask for someone to come through who is a good communicator and who will be easily recognised. Good demonstrations can be spoiled if the recipient isn't sure who the communicator is or doesn't know much about them (for example, a grandparent who died before the recipient was born).

As you put your request up to spirit, you may get a feeling of who is going to come through. However, ask them just to hold back for a moment or two, until you are on your feet, because the information needs to be – and to sound – spontaneous.

When you stand up

Smile. Look confident. Believe that you're going to be good, and you will be. Greet the audience. Give a brief introduction – particularly if they've not heard you work before. If it's not a spiritually minded audience, you may want to explain the relevance of mediumship to our lives and to say something about spirit. Make sure that your introduction is appropriate to your audience – an introduction in a church will be quite different from that at a 'psychic night' in a room above a pub. Get people thinking about their loved ones in spirit, by telling them how pleased you are to be there to help them connect with friends and family who have passed over. This will create energy. If, without speaking for too long, you can say something to make the audience laugh this, too, will raise the energy in the hall.

Tell them how you work and remind them just to answer with "yes", "no", or "I don't know". Then register your intent with spirit and allow yourself a moment to get fully into your power. Throw your power out so it fills the whole room and move your mind to spirit. It can take up to 20 seconds or so to become aware of who is with you, so don't rush to start speaking. Allow your energy to blend with that of the spirit. Sian Wilson, who used to teach on SNUi, would talk about "putting the communicator on like an old jacket". In other words, allow yourself to feel immersed in who he or she is, rather like an actor 'getting lost' in the character he is playing. And as soon as the information starts to come in, begin to speak.

A contact should take no more than five to ten minutes so, if you're the only demonstrator, that means about six to eight contacts in an hour. It's important to ask spirit for a variety of communicators – if they're all distressing, emotional and hard-hitting, the audience will go home feeling traumatised, no matter how uplifting the messages may have been.

Don't let your energy drop by letting one contact go before you look for the next. Use the energy of the first to bring in the second. If you watch the tutors demonstrate at AFC you will notice that, even if they pause for a sip of water, they go straight into a new contact after finishing the previous one.

Audience response

Working in public can be quite different from working in a circle or at AFC. At AFC, or in a closed circle, you're working with people you know, who understand what mediumship is all about. They will respond appropriately when asked to and will be willing you to do well. This may not happen in a public demonstration. Even in churches there may be members of the congregation who "know what they like" in a medium and are suspicious of anybody new, especially if he or she is introduced as a fledgling. Hopefully, this doesn't happen too often, but I have been told of instances when it has.

Equally, there may be people who don't want a message – they may be newcomers who have come simply to find out what Spiritualism is about or they may be regulars who come just for the company and to listen. So it's important in a church, once you've placed your contact, to ask the recipient if you can work with them, before continuing.

In a public demonstration in a hall or in pub, things are quite different as most people come hoping they'll get a message. However, a lack of understanding can cause enormous confusion, which is why it's particularly important to explain, before you start, exactly what it is that a medium does. A couple of AFC tutors tell stories of public demonstrations where the information has been hesitantly accepted by someone in the audience who then goes on to say "But it can't be him, because he's dead."

People have all sorts of reasons why they don't put their hands up or are hesitant. Sometimes they're just shy and will only accept the information as you're on the point of letting the link go. A year or two back I brought through someone who I knew was a mother wanting to speak to her daughter. I gave some information and asked where I was. No response. I felt a tug to one side of the room and said "I feel I'm with someone over here." Still no response. So, keeping my eyes directed to the area where I was sure my recipient was, I asked "Can anybody take the information relating to someone who wasn't their mother?" Very tentatively, a woman put her hand up. "How much of it can you take?" I asked. "All of it" she replied. I heaved a sigh of relief. "So," I said, "You can take everything apart from her being your mother." "Oh no," she said. "She was my mother."

Another reason why someone may not put up her hand is because it's too emotional – maybe she had not expected to get a message or maybe the communicator has never been through before and she's not ready for it.

If you get to the point where you've done your best and there is still no one accepting the evidence, let the contact go and say "Well if someone remembers later on who this might be, just know that he (or she) was here."

Something you may have to face in a public demonstration which, hopefully, would never happen in a church is hecklers. It's vital to deal with them in a calm and dignified way. If you can't get them to shut up after asking them nicely a couple of times, sit down and tell the organiser that you will only continue after the hecklers have left the hall. This usually results in the organiser, together with several members of the audience getting up to escort the hecklers out.

Another situation that is unconnected with your actual mediumship is that someone in the audience is taken ill. Because you're on your feet and in tune with the energies in the room, you may well be the first person to notice if someone faints or seems to be having a heart attack. Never assume that someone else will go to their aid – everyone else may be completely focused on you! Pause your communication and ensure that the person gets the help he or she needs. Spirit will understand and your communicator will still be there when you come back.

Occasionally, someone will come up to you after a demonstration where you've failed to place a link and will say "I think you had my dad up there when you were talking about . . ." They've had their chance and you're now off duty so never try to give them any more information than they've already had. Just say something along the lines of "Well, know that your dad was there."

Someone may also come up to tell you they've remembered something they said "no" to earlier. Again, don't take it any further – just thank them for telling you and say that you're glad they remembered.

Some days you will be on fire and every link will hit its mark and be joyfully accepted. Other days will be less good. Simone Key tells a story of a demonstration very early on in her career as a working medium which was so bad that she nearly gave up. Fortunately, she decided to continue and has proved herself to be not just a great medium but a wonderful teacher as well.

There's no such thing as a perfect message and we all tend to remember what went badly in a demonstration, rather than what went well. Indeed, because there tends to be an element of entrancement when we give our very best messages, these will be the ones that we remember least clearly. So, really, we're not the best people to judge! The recipients of the messages will remember everything you got right – and even if you've touched just one person, it will have been worthwhile.

12
PRIVATE READINGS & SPIRITUAL ASSESSMENTS

PRIVATE READINGS

Even if you're one of those mediums who enjoys demonstrating and isn't too fond of working one-to-one, it's worth doing some private readings because, as the late great AFC tutor Glyn Edwards used to say, private sittings are the best way to sharpen your mediumship.

Quite a few of the clients who come to you for private readings will never have seen a medium before, so it's vital not only to tell them what you're offering but also to find out what they're expecting. Some will have come for psychic readings, wanting to know why their lives have being going wrong recently and how they can take control again. However, if they want you to tell their fortunes, foretell the future or give them the numbers that will win next week's lottery, be polite but firm, tell them that's not what you do, wish them well and send them on their way!

If a client wants to hear from a specific person in spirit, it's important to explain that, while this may be possible, you can't guarantee it, because it's spirit that decides who comes through.

Some clients may be very nervous, so do your best to make them feel at ease because that will allow them to be more receptive. Having a rose quartz crystal in the room may help, but avoid incense or other scents as some people are allergic to these. Just be positive, warm and confident and take time to build a rapport.

Ensure that you have answered any questions the sitter has and that you have alleviated any fears he or she has about the process before you start. It is a good idea to ask about any hopes or expectations for a particular person to come through in order to avoid getting to the end only for the sitter to say "Well, I really wanted to hear from my mum". Occasionally a sitter may mention someone and suddenly that spirit is there. But be careful. If we rush in too soon in an attempt to bring a particular person through, there is a danger that we will be getting the information psychically from the sitter. So be very certain that you really do have that person there before you start to speak about him or her.

Just before you start, explain to your sitters how you would like them to respond to what you say. Then tell them that you won't look directly at them all the time because you don't want to be influenced by their body language. Sitting sideways in relation to your sitters, rather than straight on, will also help to avoid a solar-plexus to solar-plexus energetic link which could draw your focus into their feelings and emotions, rather than letting you concentrate on the link with spirit.

If you have been asked for a psychic reading, ask which area of her life the sitter would like you to look at, and then focus on that. If you've been asked for a mediumistic reading, spend a few minutes at the start by doing a more general psychic reading. This will allow the client to relax as you show clearly that you know what you're doing and that you understand why he is here. Project your energy towards the sitter and try to get a sense of what has been happening that has resulted in a request for a sitting. Has there been a recent bereavement or other loss? Have there been events with an emotional impact? You can't get anything in a psychic reading that the sitter doesn't want you to know, so never feel that you are prying, but rather that you are finding out about them so that you can help them to get what they need.

Explain to the sitter where you will be getting your information from (ideally without using the word psychic): "I'm going to start by having a look at your energies". Then, when you move into mediumship say "And now I'm going to make contact with the spirit world and see who's there".

Ensure that you are detached energetically from the sitter before you start to link to spirit so as not to be affected by her hopes or desires, or her negative energies if you bring through the 'wrong' person.

While you will probably be able to bring through two or three communicators during a private reading, it's important to deal fully with one before going on to the next. As in a demonstration, you first have to ensure that the sitter recognises who the person is. If, despite a good description, the link can't be taken, try asking spirit for something specific that will help the sitter to recognise who this is. If, after this, the person still isn't recognised, it may be best to ask the contact to step to one side and invite someone else in. Sometimes people expect only their nearest and dearest to come through so that the person who taught them English when they were eleven or who worked in the same office when they were twenty may not immediately be recognised (even if you are able to get the relationship) – but memories of the person may return later.

A similar problem may arise if the contact is recognised but the information is sparse or mundane or non-specific. In this case, tell the sitter that you're going to move on to someone who's a better communicator, and ask spirit to send such a person in.

If, however, you get ten minutes into the reading and the client hasn't been able to accept anything, you should stop and give a refund. It's important to note that, if you're unwell or your energy is low, your readings aren't going to be as good as when you're well, so if you get a couple of poor readings in succession it may be an indication that you need to take a break and look after yourself.

However, assuming that you are fighting fit and are getting good contacts that the sitter can take, it's still important to remain in control of the reading. Some clients may want the communicator to give them advice on what they should do about certain situations in their lives. Be very careful about this. I have heard many AFC tutors say that spirit will never tell sitters what to do but will simply support them as they find their own solutions. Do not allow clients to railroad you into asking spirit for advice about something or for permission to do something. Our first responsibility is to spirit and we need to work according to their way of doing things. In addition, giving advice (even if it does seem to come from spirit) can open you up to all sorts of problems if the results of a client acting on that advice are unsatisfactory, and you could find yourself being sued for having told him that spirit thinks he should get divorced or change his job or move to Timbuctoo, or whatever it happens to be.

A private reading is, in many ways, similar to a demonstration as far as the evidence and message is concerned. It should not consist of random facts but should tell a story and should show that the communicator is still involved in the person's life. This latter part is especially important for clients who have recently been bereaved.

When you get to the message (which should take no more than a quarter of the time given to the evidence) it should be entirely about spirit and their involvement with the sitter.

If, by the end of the reading, the requested communicator hasn't come through, don't say that she wasn't there but simply that you weren't able to tune into her.

Occasionally, you may get a client who won't respond with just "yes", "no" or "I don't know" and who seems more anxious to tell you about her loved ones than to hear about them from you. In such a case, don't fight it. Give what information you can, and allow the client to talk. And, hopefully, she'll go away thinking she's had a wonderful reading.

Practicalities of the Private Reading

Rarely, clients may become angry if you say that you can't offer them what they want (such as fortune telling), or because of something said during the reading or because the person they want to hear from doesn't come through. For all these reasons, it is important that (unless you are doing your readings at a psychic fair or similar public venue) you ensure that you are sitting closer to the door than your client so, if necessary, you can make a quick escape.

Get payment before you start. Sometimes, particularly if it's been a very emotional session, it's all too easy to forget to ask for payment at the end! Some mediums, psychics and healers feel they shouldn't charge because they're using a natural gift. But then, so too is a concert pianist, or an actor, or a singer, or a talented sportsman – and they all get paid. In addition, the money you make is your education fund – it enables you to go to courses (and to buy books such as this one!). Another reason for charging is that, if you don't, a lot of people will feel they're taking advantage of you and won't come back, while other people will think that you can't be very good, and won't come at all.

It can be helpful to have a list of resources and helplines that you can give the client if appropriate – particularly bereavement organisations and qualified local counsellors (the best place to find qualified registered counsellors in the UK is on counselling-directory.org.uk).

Before you start, tell your client how long the reading will last – and don't exceed this. Keeping to time limits doesn't restrict you, but it does help you to focus. And don't allow a client to persuade you to go on for longer because, if you do, she'll expect the same thing next time. An easy way to deal with a client who wants more is just to say "I'm sorry, the energy's gone."

Don't book readings so that they're immediately one after the other. Allow yourself some time between them, so you can go to the loo, have a cup of coffee, eat something, or whatever else you need physically and, even more important, so you can allow your energy and your mind a few minutes to recover.

Don't see clients too often. If they've recently been bereaved, once a month is OK, otherwise it shouldn't be more than once or twice a year. It's not unknown for people to become addicted to readings and gradually to get to the point where they won't do anything without guidance from spirit, through a medium. Not seeing clients too frequently also ensures that your readings don't become repetitive. At AFC, we all get numerous readings through the week from the people we're working with in the class. And, in my experience, almost invariably, the messages are very similar. (Last time I was there, the vast majority of those that I got – from a variety of communicators – were telling me to get on and finish writing this book!) So seeing people only once in a while should mean that you are able to give fresh information and messages each time.

It is a good idea to have the client sign a paper, before you start, to say that she understands that mediumship is always in the nature of an experiment, that nothing can be guaranteed, and that no major decisions should be taken that are based solely on what has been said in a reading. It's also a good idea to record the reading as this will allow the client to relax more, as she won't have to remember everything that's been said. You should keep a copy of the recording, too, (to protect yourself on the rare occasions when the client later accuses you of saying something that you didn't – and wouldn't – say).

SPIRITUAL ASSESSMENTS

The point of a spiritual assessment is to help someone who has already started to develop his or her spiritual skills. It can help to reassure someone who is uncertain whether he is on the right path, to show someone where her gifts lie, or to help someone who is struggling to move on.

It starts with a psychic reading of the spiritual layer of the client's aura and then the medium contacts the client's guides and asks them for insight and advice on his spiritual progress.

Doing assessments can be very satisfying. Some time ago, at AFC, I did an assessment for one of the other students. I had got to know her quite well during the week and we had talked a lot, so I thought I knew the sort of thing I would find. But it was very, very different. She had abilities – and was facing challenges – far greater than I could have imagined and I was astonished at what her aura and her guides revealed to me. It was an emotional experience for both of us and I felt greatly privileged that this information (which she had shared with very few people) had been shared with me.

When you tune into the aura, look at the client's energy – how vibrant is it? If there's a sluggishness, what is causing it? Then look at her relationship with spirit – is she comfortable working with spirit or does she still have anxieties about her own abilities or about where this is taking her? If your client is very young or has only recently started to develop her spiritual gifts, look at what started her off and how committed she is.

Next, look at where her gifts lie – in demonstrating, trance, healing, teaching or whatever. Which of these is strongest? One way of doing this is to visualise your sitter working. You can also find out if anything is preventing her from working to her highest potential.

Never tell anyone that he *should* be doing something or that he *can't* do something, simply because you don't see it in his aura. It may be there but you're not able to see it because it's something that he's not yet ready for. If a client asks outright, for example, "Can I become a healer?" and you can't see it, the best reply is something along the lines of "I don't see it in your aura at the moment, so maybe that's something for the future." And then go on to tell him what you *can* see and how he might develop it.

Never try to suggest a life purpose or a full plan of action. Spirit will only ever tell you your next step. Give as much detail as you can, though. For example, if you see healing, is this spiritual healing, Reiki or other form of energy healing, or does it indicate that the sitter is working as a complementary therapist, or perhaps a nurse or a doctor? If you see teaching, look to see what kind of teaching – is this running a circle for developing mediums, running workshops for different types of spiritual development, or perhaps giving talks to introduce people to the concept of using their spiritual gifts.

When you move on to link with the sitter's guides, you can say something about the guides themselves, if the sitter wants you to, but only say as much as is needed to help her to make better contact with them. Ask spirit for information that will add to and enlarge upon what you've already got from the aura. Find out what the guides feel about the sitter's development and how it's going, and about what she should do to overcome any difficulties. Find out, too, what will enhance her development and what might detract from it. But never make the sitter feel that she *has* to do something or to take a particular course of action. You may be getting indications that she should, but she may not be ready for it or may not want to do it.

A spiritual assessment should always be positive and uplifting, and the sitter should go away feeling empowered. As with private readings, clients should be discouraged from having assessments too often in order to avoid becoming reliant on them, rather than finding their own way. Once or twice a year is probably the ideal.

13

TRANCE

Before I start to write about trance, I need to make it clear that I am not (yet) a trance medium and so cannot say very much about my own experience of trance. I have done some trance training and intend to do more but for a long time I was not interested in it, preferring to concentrate on demonstrations and private readings. However, after two AFC tutors had suggested to me that it really was time that I thought about doing trance, I decided to give it a try. It was then that I discovered that one important reason for doing trance is that it can benefit your other mediumistic work. To use Leah Bond's phrase: "Trance can only enhance".

What happens in trance?

Some people are wary of trance, believing that the body of the medium is actually taken over by spirit, rather like the 'possession' depicted in horror movies. However, trance is simply an altered state of consciousness in which the guide blends with the auric field of the medium. This is just a deepening of the connection that a medium has with spirit when giving a message – but the blending in trance is much closer and therefore the information that comes through is more profound. In fact, it's the degree of blending that's all-important and not the depth of the trance.

What is most important to understand, though, is that trance is not an abnormal state but, rather, is something that comes naturally to us.

If you go to a trance course at AFC you will probably have an opportunity of sitting in a cabinet – a structure that looks rather like a sentry box or a large cupboard without a door. The function of the box is to enhance the build-up of power and to enable you to go into trance more readily.

The applications of trance

Most commonly when someone gives a trance demonstration, what we hear is their guides coming through to give us some philosophy or teaching. This can be uplifting, thought-provoking, inspiring and, sometimes, funny. But this is not the only application of trance.

Trance communication, where someone's loved one in the spirit world talks directly through the medium, is less common than it used to be but is still practised by some mediums. However, in order to do trance communication, you need to be a very experienced demonstrator as well.

Trance healing is simply what it says it is – healing while in trance. Several of the tutors at AFC offer courses on this, but it is probably best to have some experience of developing trance before trying to study trance healing. Trance itself can be very healing for the person practising it, but it can also be very emotional. I remember on one occasion sitting in a cabinet with tears pouring down my face – not because I felt sad but because I was overwhelmed by joy. On another occasion I had been feeling quite unwell all day but eight minutes sitting in a cabinet resulted in all my symptoms disappearing.

Physical mediumship is a form of trance but not everyone who can go into trance can produce physical phenomena. It is a gift that few people have, and requires a very deep level of trance and many, many years of practice. Transfiguration, where ectoplasm forms a mask-like layer in front of the medium's face, is a physical phenomenon and differs from overshadowing (where a succession of faces can be seen on a trance medium's face as the power builds). With transfiguration everyone will see the same thing, but this doesn't necessarily happen with overshadowing.

However, even those people who are not physical mediums can use trance to produce phenomena such as spirit art, automatic writing, levitation and apports (objects suddenly appearing in the room, brought by spirit from elsewhere).

The right attitude

It may sound obvious but, in order to practise trance, you have got to want to do it. One of the great trance mediums, Gladys Osbourne Leonard (who was born in 1882) had to be persuaded to start trance training and, for six months, she resisted. When she finally agreed to start, the first thing she had to do was to work to demolish the barrier she'd built up against it.

Trance doesn't come overnight, even if you are really enthusiastic about doing it. You have to be patient and you have to be committed. Like any form of mediumship, you have to find your own way of doing it – what best enables you to blend with spirit – and you need to believe that you can do it, approaching it in a calm and relaxed way. Even more, perhaps, than with demonstrating and private readings, it requires you to get to know the spirit energies, to talk to them and to build a relationship with them.

Training as a trance medium

While it is vital (as with any form of mediumship) to have good training for trance, there is a lot that you can do by yourself.

If you don't have access to a regular trance circle, you can sit on your own because the worst that can happen is that you'll go to sleep and slide off your chair (which is why it's a good idea to sit in an armchair).

There is no one set way of going into trance, but I have been shown three techniques:

- 'Magnetic' passes. This is where another medium passes her hands in a certain way over the trance medium's head. I've had experience of this and was surprised at how well it worked. However, the problem here is that you may become dependent on the passes and so find you're unable to go into trance in any other way, which is limiting. (Incidentally, if you Google 'magnetic passes for trance' it will bring up a lot of references, but these all relate to hypnosis and, while hypnosis is a form of trance, it is quite different from a mediumistic trance since it turns the consciousness inwards rather than expanding it outwards.)

- Offer yourself in service to spirit, focus on your breath and then just allow yourself to surrender. Believe in yourself, trust spirit and let go.

- Better yet, combine the second method with a request to spirit to help you to get yourself out of the way. Relax and let go effortlessly, as though you were falling asleep.

In addition, as with any form of mediumship, sending love out to spirit as you go into trance is going to help you. Since surrender is a passive thing, try to avoid actively wanting to go into trance as this can be counterproductive. Let the results take care of themselves.

Be at one with the power and sit just for the love and joy of sitting which, as Eileen Davies has pointed out, is what the great physical mediums of the past used to do, focusing just on the sitting and not on the phenomena. It is the intention that is vital.

If you have practised mindfulness, you are likely to find it helpful in dealing with the flood of thoughts that may come rushing in as you're going down into trance. You just need to acknowledge that they are there, then allow yourself to go down again. You may also get a lot of pictures flashing through your mind. Again, just let them go. Once you're in trance your mind will become quiet.

As you're going down, you may feel very cold (especially round your legs) or very hot. You may feel a sensation in your throat or neck, or a pull in your solar plexus. One part of your body may feel numb or it may seem to you that your head is being stretched up and your neck elongated. You may be aware of your heart rate speeding up. Those who are able to go into a deep trance may feel tingling in their hands and feet or a tight band around their heads. Observe but don't question what is happening – just accept it. Somebody watching may notice your breathing or your skin tone change. As your spirit expands, your body may start to feel dense and heavy. Eileen Davies says that, rather than feeling that she going down into trance, it seems as though she is expanding outwards. And both she and Jose Medrado have mentioned that, when they are in trance, they feel as though they are standing behind themselves.

It's important to take time to move into the altered state, allowing the power to build. It can take a long time – don't rush it. Don't try to speak too soon – or at all, if it doesn't feel right. It's vital to get fully into trance before you start to speak because otherwise, as Eileen Davies has said, all you'll be doing is talking with your eyes shut. Only start to speak when words that you know aren't yours begin to come into your head. But do start to speak then – if you wait too long, it becomes more difficult. You may need consciously to say the first two or three sentences but then spirit will take you down further into trance so you're hardly aware of what is being said. Harry Edwards used to say that in trance, information doesn't come *from* you but passes *through* you. It's important to remain calm and allow the words to come to you, rather than trying to grasp them. Once your guide has started to speak, don't try to focus on what is being said because that may cause the guide to withdraw.

Trance is, above all, a passive way of working for the medium. If you watch a good trance medium, you'll notice that he or she remains quite still throughout the process. Occasionally in a trance circle or workshop, we see someone who starts to over-breathe, moan, thrash around or take up a strange posture while supposedly going into trance. But none of these things are to do with trance – they are simply coming from the person's mind to draw attention to herself.

If you're fortunate enough to find a trance circle you can join, or if you decide to start your own, it's important that everyone in the circle feels comfortable with everyone else. They all need to be committed and sensible and willing to work harmoniously, with no big egos. It's also important for there to be a leader and for the circle to be closed. Using the same room each time will saturate it with power, so don't move the venue unless you really have to.

Whether you're working in a circle or by yourself, you need to sit regularly. Avoid having a heavy meal beforehand, wear comfortable clothes and, if you can, play some repetitive music with deep tones (such as Tibetan chanting) before you start. Try having a candle, crystals or flowers in the room as you may find that they enhance the energies. A dim light helps, so working after sunset when the daylight is starting to fade is the best time. If you're working with others, ensure that you're not sitting too close to each other because touching someone who is in trance can cause him to be disorientated for several hours afterwards. It's also important to avoid any loud noise at the start or end of a trance, as the medium will be very sensitive. A lot of people feel tired after coming out of trance, but eating something sweet will help.

There may be times when you feel that, although you are sitting regularly, nothing is happening. But this isn't so. Spirit will be working, even if you're not aware of it. Eventually you will achieve a blending of your mind with that of spirit. And you don't have to sit for hours every day – indeed, it's best not to sit for more than an hour at a time. But even five minutes a week can help your development. In addition, practising inspirational speaking can be a very good training for trance.

The more you practise, though, the easier it will become to speak the words that come from spirit.

AND FINALLY . . .

The Arthur Findlay College - known as the world's foremost college for the advancement of spiritualism and psychic sciences - runs over 80 courses a year on mediumship, healing, trance, spirit art and related subjects. Many are for 'mixed abilities', while others are specifically for advanced students and working mediums or for beginners.

Stansted Hall
Stansted Mountfitchet
Essex CM24 8UD
United Kingdom

Website: https://www.arthurfindlaycollege.org

Telephone: 01279 813636 (UK)
              +44 1279 813636 (from outside the UK)

email: info@arthurfindlaycollege.org
             bookings@arthurfindlaycollege.org

SNUi - the online branch of the Spiritualist National Union runs a tuition programme with at least two classes a day on various aspects of spiritualism, development circles and services. For the amount of training available, the annual fee is very low (£21 at the time of writing).

Website: https://snui.org.uk

A FEW MORE LINKS:

For information about short courses on developing psychic and mediumistic skills, run by the author, contact:
info@sphinxhouse.com

To learn more about Gordon Higginson and to see videos of him working mediumistically go to: https://www.gordonhigginson.co.uk/

For more about Mary Hykel Hunt and her courses on developing intuition go to: https://www.hykelhunt.co.uk/

To find out more about Silver Birch and his teachings go to: http://www.silverbirchpublishing.co.uk

CPSIA information can be obtained
at www.ICGtesting.com
Printed in the USA
BVHW072237290120
570848BV00005B/486

9 781999 710736